GET OVER YOURSELF

Nietzsche for our times

Patrick West

SOCIETAS
essays in political
& cultural criticism

imprint-academic.com

Published in the UK by
Imprint Academic Ltd., PO Box 200, Exeter EX5 5YX, UK

Distributed in the USA by
Ingram Book Company,
One Ingram Blvd., La Vergne, TN 37086, USA

ISBN 9781845409333 paperback

A CIP catalogue record for this book is available from the
British Library and US Library of Congress

For my mother and father

Patrick West is a freelance writer based in England. Born and raised in London, he graduated from Manchester University in 1997 with an MA in Cultural History. He has written for *The Times*, *New Statesman*, *Spectator* and *The Times Literary Supplement*, among others. He is author of *Conspicuous Compassion* (Civitas, 2004) and *The Poverty of Multiculturalism* (Civitas, 2005). He is a columnist for *Spiked* online. He lives in Kent. @patrickxwest

Contents

Guide to abbreviations of Nietzsche's works

The number refers to the book's section. The exceptions are 1) *The Untimely Meditations*, which consists of four essays with numbered sections, and 2) *Thus Spoke Zarathustra*, *The Twilight of the Idols* and *Ecce Homo*, which have chapter titles, and are abbreviated in the text appropriately.

BGE — Beyond Good and Evil
BT — The Birth of Tragedy
D — Daybreak
EH — Ecce Homo
GOM — On the Genealogy of Morals
HATH — Human, All Too Human
TAC — The Antichrist
TCOW — The Case of Wagner
TJS — The Joyous Science
TOTI — The Twilight of the Idols
TSZ — Thus Spoke Zarathustra
UM — Untimely Meditations
WTP — The Will to Power

Prologue

There have been thousands of books which profess to explain what Friedrich Nietzsche said and meant. There has been no shortage of authors telling us what they think of the German philosopher. Yet *Get Over Yourself* puts matters the other way round. Rather than simply explaining his thoughts, it instead asks: what would Nietzsche make of us? What would he think of our 21st-century, digital era?

Get Over Yourself takes Nietzsche's philosophy to understand our society, and takes our society to explain his philosophy. In our age of identity politics, therapy culture, safe spaces, religious fundamentalism, virtue signalling, Twitterstorms, public emoting, dumbing down, digital addiction and the politics of envy, this book introduces Nietzsche's philosophy by putting the man in our shoes.

It concludes how Nietzsche's philosophy can make our world a better place—and we happier people.

Introduction
Get over yourself

In Monty Python's famous "philosophy football" sketch between the Germans and the Greeks, Friedrich Nietzsche is booked for arguing with the referee Confucius, accusing him of having no free will. "This is Nietzsche's third booking in four games", announces the commentator. This sketch sums up Nietzsche's spirit neatly. It encapsulates the outlook of a philosopher who professed radical individual liberty, who urged us to defy all authority and to question everyone and everything. Nietzsche railed against servitude and the values of the herd, against all received wisdom. Were he a footballer, he wouldn't merely want to score a goal, or strive to win, or defeat the opposing team. He would question the rules and very authority of the game itself.

Nietzsche's writings live on through his most famous pronouncements. Consciously or not, we all know them. "God is dead", he declared. "Live dangerously!", he exclaimed. He invented the word "Superman". "What does not kill me makes me stronger" is another of his. "In individuals, insanity is rare; but in groups, parties, nations and epochs, it is the rule." Elsewhere: "Morality is the herd-instinct in the individual." These exhortations embody his central message: that life is tough, and we should accept and embrace this reality—and then overcome it. We should take charge of our destinies, be courageous, self-governing "supermen", fearless in the face of group-think, the mentality of the herd and ideologies that stop us thinking for ourselves and truly becoming ourselves.

Today we are surrounded by Nietzschean slogans, in society and popular culture, words that echo his creed of self-empowerment and self-overcoming. "Beyond" goes the name of a David Beckham after-shave. "Break Your Limits" reads the slogan for Enertor insoles. "Go Further" pronounce adverts for Ford. On the side of cans of the energy drink Relentless there runs the communication: "The journey towards artistry and committing everything for your moment is an accolade in itself. Greatness or glory doesn't come by accident, it is earned." The fizzy drink's spiel concludes with the entreaty: "Be unwavering in your personal pursuit of greatness."

Nietzsche's anti-authoritarianism continues to be enlisted by angry teenagers seeking a figurehead in their struggle against parental and religious authority. He appeals to the eternal adolescent spirit of irreverence, gloom and thrill-seeking. In 2012 the heavy metal giants Black Sabbath released a single called *God Is Dead?*, adorned with a picture of Nietzsche on the sleeve, while "Beyond Good & Evil" is also the title of a popular action-adventure video game. We even hear echoes of Nietzsche in Harry Potter. "Lord Voldemort showed me how wrong I was", says the character Quirrell in *Harry Potter and the Philosopher's Stone* (1997), "There is no good and evil, there is only power, and those too weak to seek it" (Rowling, 1997, p. 211).

Nietzsche's thinking about the importance of struggle and mastery is much in vogue. His maxim "what doesn't kill you makes you stronger" is a favourite in boardrooms and self-help books. His philosophy of acceptance, daily battles and becoming a better version of oneself prevails and in drug and alcohol recovery programmes. He has become an unlikely inspiration for the self-help industry. One of the most influential books of our era is Susan Jeffreys' *Feel the Fear And Do It Anyway*, a title that is pure Nietzsche. As a consequence of its success, people now enthuse about the "gift of failure" and the idea that "failure is a conduit to fearlessness". *The Stress Test: How pressure can make you stronger* (2016) by Ian Robertson is openly indebted to Nietzsche's beliefs that only by accepting hardship, and by overcoming failure, can we triumph in life.

Friedrich Nietzsche has had universal appeal since his death in 1900. He inspired some of the greatest artists of the 20th century. Freud, Camus, D.H. Lawrence, George Bernard Shaw, W.B. Yeats and Thomas Mann are among the writers who openly owe a debt to him, as are the philosophers Martin Heidegger, Carl Jung, Michel Foucault and Jacques Derrida. His influence in universities and schools and beyond has been formidable. Generations of today's teachers, policy makers and journalists have been taught first-, second- and third-hand Nietzsche's philosophy that "there is no truth, only interpretation".

He is a thinker for all people. Progressives and those on the Left venerate him for his invectives against capitalism, the nation state and bourgeois civilisation. Conservatives and Right-wingers are drawn to his muscular individualism, shameless elitism and denunciation of egalitarianism. He has been claimed by anarchists, feminists, atheists, libertarians, conservatives, postmodernists, socialists, Thatcherites, egalitarians and queer theorists. There seems to be no political movement, no school of thought, that hasn't lifted his words at some time. "Tell me what you need, and I'll supply you with the right Nietzsche quotation", once quipped the German satirist Kurt Tucholsky (Safranski, 2003, p. 11).

His wide appeal to anyone means, in turn, he has the capacity to annoy everyone. "He gets upon everybody's nerves, he fits in nowhere", wrote an early English devotee, Anthony Ludovici, in 1908. "He was, of course, a Conservative, but a severer Conservative than anyone we have known hitherto. He was, besides, a revolutionary, but a more thorough revolutionary than all the wildest revolutionaries put together" (Ludovici, 1908; 1905; 1911; 1927, pp.

vii–viii). Nietzsche's broad appeal owes to the fact that his writings are so literary, unsystematic, scatter-gun and often superficially contradictory. The philosopher Karl Jaspers advised that no one should accept any advice in Nietzsche's work until finding another passage that contradicted it. Only then could the reader decide what he really meant. No wonder Nietzsche means different things to different people. No wonder also that his writing lends itself so easily to misinterpretation.

Thus, he remains a target of vilification. In the *Closing of the American Mind* (1987), Allan Bloom complained that Nietzsche was the ultimate source of abject student nihilism, the fount of the corrosive culture of relativism eating away at the values of liberal democracy. "Nobody really believes in anything anymore, and everyone spends his life in frenzied work and frenzied play so as not to face the fact, not to look into the abyss. Nietzsche's call to revolt against liberal democracy is more powerful and more radical than is Marx's" (Bloom, 2008, p. 143).

Bloom speaks from the traditional Left, but from the opposite side, in *Experiments Against Reality* (2000), the thinker Roger Kimball typifies complaints by conservatives. He damns "Nietzschanism for the masses, as squads of cozy nihilists parrot his ideas and attitudes. Nietzsche's contention that truth is merely 'a moveable host of metaphors, metonymies, and anthropomorphisms,' for example, has become a veritable mantra in comparative literature departments across the country" (Kimball, 2000, p. 193). More recently, Peter Watson opens his 2014 work *The Age of Nothing* with the following questions on the book's very first page: "Is There Something Missing in Our Lives? Is Nietzsche to Blame?" (Watson, 2016, p. 1).

For good or bad, his admirers and detractors agree that he was a dangerous character. Nietzsche, wrote the art critic and philosopher Arthur C. Danto in 1965, has "a not altogether undeserved reputation as an intellectual hooligan, as the spiritual mentor of the arty and the rebellious" (Danto,

1965, 70, p. 13). The novelist Will Self calls him a "punk philosopher" (BBC documentary "Human, All Too Human", 1999). Like the punks, he wasn't especially political and he didn't have many positive suggestions—rather, he preferred to stick two fingers up to everybody. Yet he was more than just an intellectual hooligan or punk philosopher. He was also a great artist, one of the finest exponents of the German language. His writings are works of devastating beauty, even in translation.

Nietzsche's declared mission was "to philosophise with a hammer", and his books batter the reader even before you open the front page, bearing such bombastic titles as *Beyond Good and Evil*, *The Anti-Christ*, *Twilight of the Idols* and *Human, All Too Human*. Nietzsche's prose is at once ferocious and euphoric, sulphureous then dazzling. It is exuberant and anarchic, leering violently from the malicious to the vivacious from one sentence to the next. He breaks into French, Italian and Latin without warning and without explanation.

"His very style is tragic and heavy with the rustle of prophets' robes. His voice now rises to a loud exultant shout, and now drops to the sibilant hiss of the arch conspirator", wrote one early British disciple in 1906. "Out of the oppressive thunder-cloud of his thought come shooting at every moment splendid bright aphorisms like forked lightning; they are his thunderbolts carefully forged and shaped and sharpened" (Orage, 1906, pp. 14–15). More demurely, as one British detractor observed in 1917: "His paradoxes and even his blasphemies are the difficult effort of a child trying to be naughty" (Figgis, 1917, p. 248). Indeed: Nietzsche often writes like a high-spirited revolutionary or uninhibited adolescent, littering his prose with italics—which in quoted passages here *are all his own*—with ellipsis … and exclamation marks!

He writes with bellicosity and rapture, becoming ever more violent and apocalyptic the nearer he approaches madness, which struck him in January 1889. Consider his invectives against Christianity in *The Anti-Christ*, written only months beforehand. Here he talks of Rome "ruined by cunning, secret, invisible, anaemic vampires". Of Christianity, he continues: "This underhanded bigotry, conventicle secrecy, gloomy concepts such as Hell, such as the sacrifice of the innocent, such as the *unio mystica* in blood-drinking, above all the slowly stirred-up fire of revengefulness." He concludes with the thunderous fanfare: "I call Christianity the *one* great curse, the *one* great intrinsic depravity, the *one* great instinct for revenge which no expedient is sufficiently poisonous, secret, subterranean, *petty* — I call it the *one* immortal blemish of mankind… *From today?* — Revaluation of all values!" (TAC 59, 62).

Nietzsche represents the forbidden, the blasphemous, the immoral, the mysterious and the dark. No wonder university campuses today, with their "safe spaces" and "no platforming" of speakers with offensive opinions, are fond of banning Nietzsche societies. His advice to those who sought a safe and comfortable life was: "Live Dangerously! Build your cities on the slopes of Vesuvius! Send your ships into uncharted seas! Live at war with your peers and yourselves! Be robbers and conquerors as long as you cannot be rulers and possessors, you seekers of knowledge!" (TJS 283).

By the time of his insanity in the 1890s, he had gained a reputation as a mad and bad thinker. By the first half of the 20th century, he had become a figure of utmost notoriety. His writings, infused with military metaphors and the pugnacious rhetoric of struggle, survival and insurrection, were cult reading among Europe's restless youth that were about to go to war with one another. Consequently, his reputation didn't survive the First World War intact. Some even blamed him for it. "We all know", wrote the novelist Somerset Maugham in his memoirs *The Summing Up* (1938), "how the philosophy of Nietzsche has affected some parts of the world and few would assert that its influence has been other than disastrous." Even P.G. Wodehouse enlisted Jeeves into the multitude who denounced the German. In *Carry On Jeeves* (1925), after Bertie Wooster's prospective marriage to

Lady Florence falls through, Jeeves reflects: "it was her intention to start you almost immediately upon Nietzsche. You would not enjoy Nietzsche, sir. He is fundamentally unsound" (Wodehouse, 1925, 1999, p. 24).

Worse was to come, when he was most infamously appropriated by Hitler and the Nazis. Nietzsche has the unfortunate distinction of being blamed not just for one, but for two world wars. As *The Onion* joked in *Our Dumb Century*, with the imaginary news story from September 1901, under the headline "NIETZSCHE POSITS EXISTENCE OF 'SUPER-MODELS'": "Although the works are earning great renown, some fear Nietzsche's ideas may one day be misunderstood and used to justify terrible atrocities" (Scott Dikkers (ed.), 1999, p. 3).

To be clear from the outset: Nietzsche wasn't a proto-Nazi. He loathed nationalism, militarism, anti-Semitism and group-think. He was an arch-individualist. His writings were grossly misunderstood and selectively interpreted. When he wrote of "war" he meant it metaphorically, rather than in terms of tanks and guns, and "struggle" (*Kampf*) in terms of struggle against ideas and against one's own pre-conceptions, not in terms of *Mein Kampf.*

Nietzsche detested the spirit of Prussian militarism and chauvinism of his own era. He protested that he didn't even like his own fellow countrymen, writing that "the Germans are impossible for me. Whenever I picture to myself a type of man that goes against all my instincts it always turns into a German" (EH TWC.4). He wrote witheringly of "the anti-Semites, who… seek to rouse all the bovine elements of the people through an exasperating abuse of the cheapest means of agitation and moral attitudes… that every kind of intellectual swindle achieves some degree of success in the Germany of today is linked to the virtual undeniable and already tangible *satisfaction* of the German mind, whose cause I seek in an all-too exclusive diet of newspapers, politics, beer, and Wagnerian music" (GOM 3.133; p. 133). He loathed small, resentful men such as Hitler. He baulked at the kind of mass conformity that would come to be epitomised by the rallies at Nuremberg.

Yet a highly subjective and selective approach to his many maxims and aphorisms leant itself easily to misinterpretation. Nietzsche's talk of the "Superman" and masters, his constant invectives against "degenerates", slaves, "the weak" and the feeble, could easily be taken up by racists and eugenicists. And they were. Millions would need to be cleared away, he wrote in *The Genealogy of Morals*, to let one superior breed of people prosper: "the mass of humanity sacrificed to the flourishing of a single *stronger* species of man—now that *would* be progress" (GOM 2.12).

His language is indisputably bellicose. His name was even mentioned at the Nuremberg trials in January 1946: "His vision of the masses being governed without constraints by the rulers presaged the Nazi regime. Nietzsche believed in the supreme race and the primacy of Germany in which he saw a young soul and inexhaustible reserves" (Sautet & Boussignac, 1990, p. 189). That same year, in his landmark *History of Western Philosophy*, Bertrand Russell wrote damningly that "partly as a result of his teaching, the real world has become very like his nightmare" (Russell, 1946, 1962, p. 735). Thus from the Great War until the 1960s Nietzsche's name remained an abomination in universities and in public discourse, especially in the English-speaking world. As a leading Nietzsche scholar of the late 20th century, J.P. Stern, reflected in 1978: "'Mad genius... evil Teuton... satanic mind', were words applied by a respectable critic to Nietzsche when I first wrote about him more than twenty-five years ago..." (Stern, 1978, 1985, p. 22). Even by the 1970s Nietzsche's fortunes were in swift reversal. He is now revered, and still reviled, as one of the most influential thinkers of modern times. Literally thousands of books have been written about him.

So what makes this one different? *Get Over Yourself* not only looks at how Nietzsche helped to shape Western society today, for good or ill, but why he remains a popular figure.

But it's more than just an introduction and guide to his thoughts and writings. Countless books continue to discuss, question or explain Nietzsche's philosophy, but a more interesting question is to ask: what would Nietzsche make of us? It's all speculation on my behalf, of course. It is my subjective judgement, based on my readings and interpretation of his work, coloured by my own prejudices. But Nietzsche, that champion *par excellence* of personal interpretation and person creation, would have it no other way. In this spirit, *Get Over Yourself* ponders what Nietzsche would make of our society.

Nietzsche was a prophet of moral revolution, of destruction of all that is decadent and life-negating. He preaches liberation, originality, reinvention and self-creation. He championed a curious brew of radical, aristocratic individualism and the dawn of a new type of man, liberated from old, herd-like superstitions of Christianity or earthbound ideologies such as socialism or humanism. He preaches the *Übermensch* — variously translated as the "above man", "beyond man" or "superman" (there is no single English word corresponding to the German *über*; to complicate things further, *Mensch* means "person", not the gender specific "man") — the figure who goes beyond those around him and surpasses what he once was. Nietzsche challenged prejudices and received opinions, both of others and those that we find in ourselves. We must forever struggle and strive. The Superman becomes a better version of himself, always and ever.

The 21st century has witnessed the dawn of the new digital age of hyperconnectivity, censorship on campuses, religious fundamentalism and populism in politics against the elites. It's an age in which Nietzsche's ideas are more relevant than ever. He was a radical individualist who scorned the base thinking of groups, who spurned resentment and ideologies. If Nietzsche would have lamented the expansion of democracy since his death, he would have been aghast at the power of social media and its incessant chatter.

In an age of Twitterstorms, his words on the dangers of the mob are pertinent. He would have agreed that we were indeed in need of "digital detox", esteeming as he did quiet and solitude.

"Live dangerously" is a declaration that students of today with their "safe spaces" and books with "trigger warnings" would do well to take heed. He wrote about the aggressive morality of self-proclaimed victims, which we should bear in mind when people complain of "micro-aggressions" or inveigh about being "offended" and their feelings hurt. We shouldn't shy from dangerous words or dangerous ideas. The self-righteous with their firmly-held beliefs are the enemies of civilisation. Instead, we should have "dangerous spaces" where everything is questioned.

His diatribes against organised religion and its claims are never more relevant in our age of violence at the behest of religious fanatics. Islamist terrorists are the embodiment of the feeble, resentful type full of envy, bitterness and righteousness. The people with God, or good, on their side are always the worst, Nietzsche believed. Religion cultivated convictions, and it is people with firm convictions who are responsible for life's woes. This applied to all who held to ideology, sacred or secular. "Convictions are more danger-ous enemies of truth than lies" (HATH 483), he wrote in *Human, All Too Human*. It's a sentiment echoed and made more famous by the poet W.B. Yeats, one of the first and most influential of Nietzsche's disciples, in *The Second Coming*: "The best lack all conviction, while the worst / Are full of passionate intensity." Nietzsche scorned all those possessed with solid certitudes, who forgot the value of doubt.

Nietzsche defamed Christianity because he believed it made people profoundly unhappy. It placed emphasis on happiness in a promised afterlife and thus legitimised an impoverished one in the here and now. This is because Christianity emerged as a religion for slaves in the Roman Empire. This helpless and oppressed class who first took up

Christianity could never hope to overthrow their powerful masters, so they resorted to justifying their miserable existence with the consolation of a paradise hereafter. In doing so, Christianity came to venerate poverty, humility, meekness, turning states of powerlessness into virtues. This also entailed defaming the powerful, turning once noble virtues into sins. Powerlessness becomes "goodness", submission becomes "obedience", baseness becomes "humility", impotence in the face of those who have aggrieved you becomes "forgiveness". The Christian, he wrote, "sullies and suspects the beautiful, the splendid, the rich, the proud, the self-reliant, the knowledgeable, the powerful" (WTP 250). Christianity taught us to be small.

Socialism was no better, said Nietzsche. It was Christianity without the god. It promised a better life in the future, demanding thus we all be equal in the present. If Christianity taught us we were all equal before God, the egalitarianism of socialism and humanism also prevented distinctions arising in society, of levelling everyone down, of preventing the excellent from fulfilling their potential. This Christian-begotten culture which recoils at hierarchy, and thereby encourages mediocrity, is still with us. He would thus, for example, take issue with "grade inflation" in exams, the notion that "everyone is a winner" in the school playing fields or positive discrimination in the workplace. Nietzsche believed that some people are better than others and should be allowed to achieve their goals. In the quarrel about private versus state education, he wouldn't sneer at public schools. That would be life-negating envy at work. He would urge state schools to become better than their fee-paying rivals.

Nietzsche believed that European culture in the 19th century was decadent. He espoused a philosophy of nobility that was against egalitarianism, believing the latter fostered a spirit of mediocrity. This cry still resonates with contemporary complaints of "dumbing down" in our own culture. He would find cultural relativism risible. He would be appalled at the reluctance in the West to defend our own values, the mantra that "all cultures are equal" or the decrying of authors because they happen to be white and male and dead.

Nietzsche inveighed against public displays of conspicuous compassion designed to make participants feel superior about themselves, and to intimidate dissenters. He would thus have much say about the outpouring of public grief after the death of Princess Diana, the "virtue signalling" of today and the wearing of large remembrance day poppies as early as September to draw attention to your own public virtuousness. Ostentatious self-pity is merely infantile attention-seeking. As he wrote in *Human, All Too Human*: "observe how children weep and cry, so that they will be pitied, how they wait for the moment when their condition will be noticed... Thus the thirst for self-pity is a thirst for self-enjoyment, and at the expense of one's fellow man" (HATH 50).

Nietzsche believed not in being, but in doing. Change, not stasis, was the essence of existence. He baulked at introspection and the idea that we should "know ourselves". Instead, he said, we should perpetually recreate ourselves — onwards and upwards. He would have laughed at identity politics and those who guard their "sense of self" against perceived slights. He would have mocked at the impulse to give ourselves new labels and our fixation with identities. He rejected the idea that we are fixed beings, able to be pigeon-holed. He believed that we are in a constant state of flux, recreating ourselves and in perpetual struggle with others and ourselves. True honesty not only involves waging war against the opinions of others, but declaring war upon ourselves and our own views. Everything must be questioned. "The great man is necessarily a skeptic... Freedom from any kind of conviction is part of the strength of his will" (WTP 963).

The fundamental lesson from Nietzsche is that life is eternal struggle and overcoming. And this is a good thing.

Only through embracing adversity and conflict will we eventually find joy. We complain of "stress" in the workplace or classroom. He would suggest that there is no problem here. We should welcome adversity in order to overcome it. We should throw away introspective self-help books and just get on with life by challenging it, daring it, conquering it. Happiness is not a goal to be aimed for. It's a consequence of what we do. In Friedrich Nietzsche's work, we find not only a titanic thinker who would make a devastating critique of Western culture in the 21st century, but a man who can inspire us all to become who we can be and want to be. Don't think. Just do it. Dare to become someone you feared you'd never be.

Today there is much resentment towards the super-rich, bankers or other people who make us think lesser of ourselves. Much of this is legitimate. Casino capitalists deserve our ire. Your friends on Facebook who seem to have a better life than you do sometimes drag you down. But Nietzsche would say to all this fruitless rancour and complaining: Envy is a corrosive emotion that will eat you up. Resentment, jealousy and self-pity will take you nowhere. Don't resent the rich, become rich yourself. Don't envy the success of others: be a success yourself. Don't resent others. Be better than them.

This is a difficult message to accept. But that's his whole point. His message is that life is hard. As he wrote in his swansong, *Ecce Homo*: "Every conquest, every step forward in knowledge, is the outcome of courage, of hardness towards one's self, of cleanliness towards one's self" (EH: Preface.3). Avoid becoming resentful, envious or self-pitying. Life is struggle. Become your own master. Get over yourself.

Human, all too human

The life of Friedrich Nietzsche

To understand the philosophy of Friedrich Nietzsche one has to know his life, a life itself characterised by pain, struggle, rejection, disappointment, ostracism and exile. We can well believe it when Nietzsche writes that all philosophy is subjective and a projection of the self, for his own life and his views on it were intimately linked.

Friedrich Wilhelm Nietzsche was born in the Saxon village of Röcken on October 15, 1844, to Carl Ludwig Nietzsche and Franziska Nietzsche, and into a family steeped in religion. His mother was the daughter of a Lutheran minister and his father was himself a pastor in the Lutheran church. Nietzsche's paternal grandfather and namesake was author of several books including *Gamaliel, or the Everlasting Duration of Christianity: For Instruction and Sedation* (1796). The young Friedrich liked to believe that the Nietzsches hailed from Polish nobility, although there is no evidence for this. Rather, he came from the *petit rentier* middle classes, and his ancestors weren't nobles but had been butchers. Fritz's first four years, as he later recalled, "flowed on smoothly like a bright summer day", before his father died of a brain disease after months of agony and mental confusion. A few months later Nietzsche's baby brother, Joseph, also died. By the age of five, Nietzsche had, he said, put "joy and happiness" behind him.

Young Friedrich was henceforth raised in Naumburg in a house comprised entirely of women: his mother, his younger sister Elisabeth, a maternal grandmother and two maiden aunts. At the age of 13 he was sent to a top private boarding school in Pforta where he was immersed in Greek literature. He was a serious and pious youth, teased at school by boys who nicknamed him "the little pastor". "In Anglo-Saxon countries, he would have been a horrible prig", is one later verdict of the teenage Nietzsche (Brinton, 1948, p. 8). Such ostracism gave him early exposure to the power of herd-thinking and judgement, awakening the spirit of the individual in struggle against the world. He later claimed that "as a 13-year-old boy I was already preoccupied with the problem and origin of evil" (GOM 1.3), and during his high school and college years from 1858 to 1868 he penned nine autobiographical sketches, each on the general theme of "How I became what I am" (Safranksy, 2002, p 25).

In 1864 at the age of nineteen he went to the University of Bonn to study theology and classic philology, with a view of following his father's footsteps into the church. The serious, solitary youth initially tried to ingratiate himself into typical student life, taking to drinking, fighting a duel (from which he received scar on his nose) and joining a fraternity. But he soon found himself revolted by its unclassical, unsophisticated, beer-drinking patriotism and "outrageous philistinism", noting: "This unexaltedness, this ponderous clumsiness, this humdrum, pedestrian mentality, this arid sobriety which reveals itself most hideously in drunkenness" (cited in Cate, 2002, p. 51). From now on the pious, earnest Nietzsche would retain an aversion to alcohol, reflecting later: "Alcoholic drinks are no good for me; a glass of wine or beer a day is quite enough to make life for me a 'Vale of Tears'" (EH WIASC.1).

At Bonn he discovered David Strauss's *The Life of Jesus* (*Das Leben Jesu*) and Daniel Schenkel's *The Character and*

Image of Jesus (*Das Charakterbild Jesu*), both of which were revolutionary in that they treated Jesus as an historical figure and a human being (Santaniello, 2001, p. 141). His faith was broken. Upon returning home after one semester, Nietzsche refused to take communion and announced he would not be entering the church. In 1865 he dropped theology and switched to Leipzig University, where he concentrated on philology. Although the study of ancient texts had a tangible and lasting influence, he would soon lose interest in this discipline, too, having that autumn chanced upon in a second-hand bookshop an edition of Arthur Schopenhauer's *The World as Will and Representation* (*Die Welt als Wille und Vorstellung*). He was immediately transfixed.

> I took the unfamiliar book in my hands and began leafing through the pages. I don't know what demon it was that whispered in my ear: "Take this book home." So, breaking my principle of never buying a book too quickly, I did just that. Back home, I threw myself into the corner of the sofa with my new treasure, and began to let that dynamic gloomy genius work on my mind… I found myself looking into a mirror which reflected the world, life and my own nature with terrifying grandeur… Here I saw sickness and health, exile and refuge, Hell and Heaven. (cited in Hollingdale, 1985, p. 36)

Schopenhauer's view that life consists of suffering and thus necessitated consequent escape and renunciation appealed to Nietzsche. So did Schopenhauer's readable, literary prose, which contrasted starkly to contemporary mainstream German philosophy, that of Kant and Hegel, with its arcane dogma and clinical rationalising. In 1874, Nietzsche would dedicate an essay to him. Nietzsche's ideal "Schopenhauer man", he wrote, "will destroy his happiness on earth, he must be an enemy to the men he loves and the institutions in which he grew up, he must spare neither person nor thing, however it may hurt him, he will be misunderstood and thought an ally of the forces that he abhors, in his search for righteousness he will seem unrighteous by human stand-ards: but he must comfort himself with the words that his teacher Schopenhauer once used: 'A happy life is impossible, the highest thing that man can aspire to is a *heroic* life'" (UM 4 iv).

As with much that Nietzsche wrote, it was partly auto-biographical. Nietzsche's life already consisted of struggle, as from an early age he suffered from poor eye-sight, stomach pains and crippling headaches that often left him bed-ridden for days. To compound this, all of his books were commercial and critical failures in his lonely lifetime. This isolation was only partly self-inflicted. Nietzsche did seek friendship, but he wanted friends to idolise and sought perfection. Inevitably, none would meet his high expecta-tions. And following Schopenhauer's lead, Nietzsche would eventually leave academia and became an independent philosopher. Like a modern-day Socrates, rather than seek acceptance, Nietzsche sought to question that which society took for granted as normal.

It was perhaps a paradoxical path, given Nietzsche's disdain for the ancient Greek. And although Nietzsche did decry the rationalism of Socrates, which he believed killed off the wild and uninhibited spirit of Hellenic Greece, Nietzsche came to resemble Socrates. Like Nietzsche after him, Socrates taught that just because a belief is long-standing or widely held, that doesn't make it true. We shouldn't trust a belief because the masses say it is true. Tenets of belief have to stand on their own arguments. As Socrates said: "Don't you think it a good principle that one shouldn't respect all human opinions, but only some and not others... that one should respect the good ones, but not the bad ones?... we shouldn't care all that much about what the populace will say of us, but about what the expert on matters of justice and injustice will say" (Plato's Dialogues: Crito, 47a–48a; cited in de Botton, 2000, p. 34). Nietzsche, too, would find renown as a fearless trouble-maker.

In 1867, in "a fit of patriotism" (Stewart, 2011, p. 154), Nietzsche signed up for a year of voluntary service in the Prussian artillery division, distinguishing himself as a cavalry rider, before an accident in March 1868 tore two muscles in his back. Left exhausted and unable to walk for months he returned to his studies. In January 1869, at the mere age of 24, Nietzsche received an offer to become professor of classical philology at the University of Basel. In taking up the position, he renounced his Prussian citizenship, and henceforth spent his days restlessly between Switzerland, France and Italy.

He returned to the army at the outbreak of the Franco-Prussian war of 1870–71, serving as a medical orderly. Here he contracted dysentery and diphtheria, but warfare was to have a more profound effect on him. He hated army drill, which instilled in him a mistrust of authority. The patriotic pronouncements by armchair patriots at home ingrained in him a suspicion of "experts", while newspaper propaganda made him suspicious of witness accounts claiming to be "evidence" and hard truth (Hayman, 1980, p. 92). He feared for the consequences of the war, too, dreading that a German victory would encourage expansionism and triumphalism, rendering German culture more crude and vulgar. "When Nietzsche set off for the war he was stirred by patriotic ardour, filled with the vision of the splendour, heroism, and self-sacrifice of war" writes Frederick Copleston in *Friedrich Nietzsche, Philosophy of Culture* (1975). "But the result of the war, the German victory over France, made him anxious and apprehensive: he feared that 'we shall pay for our marvellous national victories at a price which I, for my part will never consent'" (Copleston, 1975, p. 9).

During his time at Basel, Nietzsche frequently visited Richard Wagner's house in Tribschen in Lucerne, having first met the composer in Leipzig through a mutual acquaintance in 1868. He idolised Wagner and had deep affection for his wife, Cosima. For her birthday in 1870 he gave her the manuscript of what was to be his first book: *The*

Birth of Tragedy (*Die Geburt der Tragödie*) in 1872. It was an analysis of Greek pre-Socratic culture, in which he speculated that the Greeks were beautiful and noble because they recognised the fundamentally terrible nature of existence, and that they had the strength to endure their suffering and render it creative through art. It was ignored by the public and damned by his colleagues on account of its speculative nature and it lost him much crediblity — although Wagner defended it.

There followed *Untimely Meditations* (*Unzeitgemässe Betrachtungen* — sometimes translated today as *Thoughts Out of Season*). This consisted of four essays published between 1873 and 1876 which challenged the triumphalism emergent in German culture after its unification and military victory in 1871. A military nation jubilant in victory would have a perilous impact on morality and art. He noted that "a great victory is a great danger. Human nature endures it with more difficulty than a defeat" (UM 1 i). The German nation-state's triumphalism would lead to the vulgarisation of its culture. The latter would become more abased the stronger and more swaggering the former became: "it threatens to convert our victory into a signal defeat. A defeat? — I should say rather, into the uprooting of the 'German Mind' for the benefit of the 'German Empire'" (UT 1 i). Only through failure are cultures spurred to evolve. Victory brings with it the temptation to lapse in to complacency and degeneration. Thus he also predicted, correctly, that defeated France would consequently flourish artistically in the latter part of the 19th century.

Nietzsche continued to mix with the Wagners, but he was profoundly disappointed by the 1876 Bayreuth Festival which he thought vulgar and bloated. He was repulsed by Wagner's increasing sense of self-importance and German chauvinism and eventually fell out with the composer. He thought Wagner had become "an old, inflexible man... His aspirations and mine keep drawing apart. This pains me considerably" (Fuss & Shapiro, 1971, p. 44). Worst of all,

Wagner had seemed to reconcile himself with Christianity. Nietzsche condemned *Parsifal* for being "all too Christian, dated, narrow-minded. All sorts of bizarre psychology. No meat and far too much blood", adding "I don't like hysterical females either" (Fuss & Shapiro, 1971, p. 42).

Nietzsche soon finally parted company with academia, too, impelled by his poor health to relinquish his chair at Basel in 1879. It was a merciful release. Academia never suited him, forever the loner and outsider, a character always bound to quarrel with institutions. He hadn't been happy at Basel, writing "I feel so alien and indifferent among the mass of my honoured colleagues that I turn down with pleasure the invitations that flow in daily. Even the enjoyment of mountains, forest, and lake is somewhat spoiled for me by the herd of my fellow-teachers" (Brinton, 1948, p. 28).

In 1879, as he explained in a letter to his publishers: "I have resigned my professorship and am going into the mountains. I am on the verge of desperation and have scarcely any hope left. My sufferings have been too great, too persistent. A HALF-BLIND MAN" (Levy, 1921, 1985, p. 121). In another letter, in a remark that foresaw his own Zarathustra figure, he stated: "I shall live in solitude for years to come, until, as a philosopher of life, ripened and ready, I dare risk (as I shall doubtless require) human intercourse again" (Fuss & Shapiro, 1971, p. 46). In 1880 he went to Genoa, where he would live a simple life on a modest pension. "Three things make up my recreation—rare recreation—my Schopenhauer, Schumann's music, and finally, solitary walks" (Brinton, 1948, p. 18). On account of his frugal living his Italian neighbours gave him the nick-name "*Il Santo*" ("The Saint").

On account of his poor health, seeking clean air, he spent seven summers in the 1880s in the village of Sils-Maria in the Swiss Alps region of Engadine. Still his health deteriorated further, Nietzsche writing to his friend and rare loyal supporter, the composer Peter Gast, "I feel like a very old man" (Copleston, 1972, p. 14). As he confided in a letter to another friend, the theologian Franz Overbeck, in June 1879: "Pain, loneliness, walks, bad weather — that is my routine. No trace of excitement. Rather a kind of mindless, stupefied indisposition" (Hayman, 1980, p. 213). Nietzsche's father had passed away at the age of 35 and Friedrich was convinced that he would also die prematurely. Yet Nietzsche's torments were his making, as physical afflictions helped to shape his writing. A man for whom life was literally an everyday struggle could not help but regard existence itself as strife, as a series of obstacles to be overcome.

If his torments inspired the message of his writings, they also helped to mould their form. Poor eye-sight prevented any long or sustained periods of continuous writing, so he would compose most of his thoughts mentally during his lengthy mountainous walks, notebook to hand, with an umbrella to protect his delicate eyes from the sun. This mode of composition accounts for the pithy, aphoristic style of his middle and later period in the 1880s, with its "wealth of trenchant epigrams and an abundance of pregnant aphorisms which the superficial may readily use as a kind of philosophical spice to be taken, a grain or two at a time, to stimulate jaded nerves", as one 1915 author observed (Wolf, 1915, p. 24). By the late 1870s Nietzsche was walking six to eight hours nearly every day. "I am always on the road two hours before the sun comes over the mountains, and especially in the long shadows of afternoon and evening", he wrote in a letter to Erwin Rohde, a fellow philologist, in August 1877 (Hayman, 1980, p. 195).

Unlike his debut *The Birth of Tragedy*, the books that follow have no structure that a systematic philosopher would recognise. They can be understood by being delved into or by returning to favourite sections (as well as being read from beginning to end). It's a method Nietzsche recommended himself in *Daybreak*: "A book such as this is not for reading straight through or reading aloud but for dipping into, especially when out walking or on a journey;

you must be able to stick your head into it and out of it again and again and discover nothing familiar to you" (D 454).

His surroundings in the mountains of Switzerland and the Italian coast were also influential and also suited his temperament. His books abound with natural imagery, of lakes, birds of prey, thunderstorms, serpents, oceans and mountains. From his youth Nietzsche had found nature inspiring, particularly when it was at its most tempestuous. "Yesterday a heavy storm hung in the sky, and I hastened up a neighbouring hill", he wrote in letter from Naumburg in 1866.

> The storm broke with a mighty crash, discharging thunder and hail, and I felt inexpressibly well and full of zest, and realised with singular clearness that to under-stand Nature one must go to her as I had just done, as a refuge from all worries and oppressions. What did man with his restless will matter to me then? What did I care for the eternal "Thou shalt" and "Thou shalt not"? How different are lightening, storm and hail—free powers without ethics! How happy, how strong they are—pure will untrammelled by the muddling influence of the intellect! (Levy, 1921, 1985, pp. 22–23)

Nature, always in constant change, represents the instability and harshness of existence. It is all amoral energy and force. "Let us beware of saying that there are laws in nature. There are only necessities: there is nobody who commands, nobody who obeys, nobody who trespasses" (TJS 109).

He was especially infatuated by mountains, a passion which can be seen in context with his preoccupation with overcoming. Mountains embody struggle. "In the mountains of truth you will never climb in vain: either you will get up higher today or you will exercise your strength so as to be able to get up higher tomorrow" (HATH II 358). Mountains represent ascending, overcoming, discovery. "Philosophy, as I have hitherto understood and lived it, is a voluntary living in ice and high mountains—a seeking after everything strange and questionable in existence, all that his hitherto has been excommunicated by morality" (EH Foreward.3). One has to ascend mountains, literally to rise above all others, through toil and struggle and setbacks and hardship. "He who climbs upon the highest mountains laughs at all tragedies, real or imaginary" (TSZ ORAW). This aphorism appears in *Thus Spoke Zarathustra* (1883–85), his most influential book that was for many years regarded as also his most important (today *On the Genealogy of Morals* is generally given that accolade, followed by *Beyond Good and Evil* and *The Joyous Science*). Nietzsche claimed that inspiration for *Zarathustra* had come to him in the Alps, "6,000 feet beyond man and time" (EH TSZ 1).

The tale, related in the style of a parody of the Bible, tells the story of the prophet Zarathustra, who after a decade alone in the mountains descends to tell man about that "God is dead". (In real life, Zarathustra, or Zoroaster, was a Persian religious teacher who lived in 7th to 6th centuries BC. In Nietzsche's book he serves as the author's spokesman and alter-ego.) Superficially, the statement is obviously non-sensical. God by definition is immortal. But Nietzsche was fond of paradoxes and of words that startled us and made the reader think. Rather than being a literal statement, "God is dead" is meant to convey the idea that the belief in a deity who gives moral authority is no more, yet we haven't noticed yet. We conduct our lives as if God's authority still held firm, carrying on as if Christian values of good and evil are self-evident.

Nietzsche's point was that in the late 19th century Western culture still unthinkingly clung to Christian morality even though it no longer held to Christianity belief, the source of our morality. A crisis of authority lay ahead. Nietzsche was warning of the forthcoming catastrophe that faced civilisation once new forms of man-made authority would begin by stealth to exert themselves in the nihilist void we were sleepwalking into. "For some time now, our whole European culture has been moving toward a catastrophe, with a tortured tension that is growing from decade to decade: restless, violently, headlong, like a river that wants to reach the end" (WTP PREF 1).

Nietzsche was no nihilist; he warned against lazy nihilism, as nihilism as an end in itself. As Albert Camus, one of Nietzsche's few defenders in the postwar era, wrote in *The Rebel* (*L'Homme révolté*; 1951): "Nietzsche never thought except in terms of an apocalypse to come, not in order to extol it, for he guessed the sordid and calculating aspect that this apocalypse would finally assume, but in order to avoid it and to transform it into a renaissance" (Camus, 2000, p. 39). Active nihilism would only be a mandatory stage for Nietzsche, after Christian morality finally collapsed, before we revalued and recreated our new system of values: "nihilism represents the ultimate logical conclusion of our great values and ideals — because we must experience nihilism before we can find out what these 'values' really had. — We require, sometime, *new values*" (WTP PREF 4).

Despite that maxim for which he is remembered, "God is Dead", Nietzsche never was a consistently dogmatic or intemperate atheist, a writer ceaselessly inveighing against the wickedness and stupidity of religion. Nietzsche was no obsessive god-denier in the mould of Richard Dawkins or Christopher Hitchens, no Oolon Colluphid (Douglas Adams' fictional author of *Where God Went Wrong, Some More of God's Greatest Mistakes* and *Who is this God Person Anyway?*) In his earlier writings, it's true, he did touch upon the inconsistencies of Christianity. "A god who is all-knowing and all-powerful and who does not even make sure that his creatures understand his intention — could that be a god of goodness?", he asked in *Daybreak*. "Would he not be a cruel god if he possessed the truth and could behold mankind miserably tormenting itself over the truth? — But perhaps he is a god of goodness notwithstanding — and merely *could* not express himself more clearly! Did he perhaps lack the intelligence to do so?" (D s91).

Yet his later writings are far more preoccupied with Christianity's negative effect on people and how it makes people have a negative mindset, to be full of sickly and guilty feelings. The debate of the existence or non-existence of a deity scarcely features. "I am too inquisitive, too incredulous, too high spirited, to be satisfied with such a palpably clumsy solution to things!" (EH WIASC.1). Nietzsche is obsessed with Christianity, to be sure, but from a psychological perspective. "The question of the mere 'truth' of Christianity — whether in regard to the existence of its God or the historicity of the legend of its origin... is a matter of secondary importance", he wrote in 1888, stressing that he was far more concerned with "the question of the value of Christian *morality*". Is it Christian morality "*worth* anything, or is it a shame and a disgrace despite all the holiness of its arts of seduction?" (WTP 251).

Nietzsche would agree with Dawkins that there is no need to disprove God, just as there is no need to disprove The Flying Spaghetti Monster. To Nietzsche, the non-existence of a Christian God was so obvious it needed no further discussion. He would never settle with the term atheist, because it suggests a settled, complacent knowledge. Atheism for him was a stage. He decried any "-ism", because that pertains to ideology and certitude. Nietzsche argued, and how he did argue, that all dogmas were to be overcome, not subscribed to.

Nietzsche's books in his most fertile period, the late 1880s, continue in this spirit of Zarathustra with growing intensity and belligerence. Such arresting names as *Twilight of the Idols, or, How to Philosophize with a Hammer (Götzen-Dämmerung, oder, Wie man mit dem Hammer philosophirt)* and *The Antichrist (Der Antichrist)* reflect Nietzsche's increasing and ever-more shrill tone. He looked the part, too. In portraits and photographs of the man, Nietzsche forever averts our gaze, his thousand-yard-stare directed elsewhere. Then there is that bristling Prussian cavalry moustache. This imposing look has always been central to his appeal and reputation. He looks the part of the philosopher who is mad, bad and dangerous to know. In his 1909 book *Egoists: A book of Superman*, James Huneker already observed that: "Thanks to the conceptions of some writers, Nietzsche and the Nietzchians are gigantic brutes, a combination of Genghis Khan and Bismarck, terrifying apparitions wearing mustachios, eyes rolling in frenzy, with a philosophy that ranged from pitch-and-toss to manslaughter, and with consuming atheism as a side attraction" (Huneker, 1909, p. 256). Yet, as is often the case with those known for their vehement and belligerent prose (Auberon Waugh, A.A. Gill, Rod Liddle, Richard Dawkins), Nietzsche was quite the opposite in real life.

Consider the opening passage of "Why I Am A Fatality", from *Ecce Homo*, a passage that predicts, it is said, the great world wars of the 20th century. "I know my fate. One day there will be associated with my name the recollection of something frightful — of a crisis like no other before on earth, of the profoundest collision of conscience, of a decision evoked *against* everything that until then had been believed in, demanded, sanctified. I am not a man, I am dynamite... there will be wars such as there have never yet been on earth" (EH WIAD.1). This was the same Nietzsche, forever struggling to get attention, who earlier confided to Rohde: "To tell the truth, I live through you; I advance by leaning upon your shoulder, for my self-esteem is wretchedly weak, and you have to assure me of my own worth again and again" (Lavrin, 1971, p. 104). Or consider an 1883 letter he wrote to Overbeck: "I no longer see why I should live for even half a year more. Everything is boring, painful, *dégoûtant*. I've suffered too much and sacrificed too much; I feel so incomplete, so inexpressibly conscious of having bungled and botched my whole creative life. It's all hopeless. I won't do anything worthwhile again. Why do anything any more!" (Fuss & Shapiro, 1971, p. 73). As he had confided in Overbeck the year before: "everything I hear makes me think that people despise me" (letter to Overbeck, 25/12/82; cited in de Botton, 2000, p. 241).

Much of his correspondence betrays a lachrymose, adolescent streak. "How wretched and loathsome it is to be me to continually wailing like a mire-drum. For the moment I am really very, very tired of everything — more than tired", Nietzsche wrote from Basel in 1874, sounding like a 19th-century version of Morrissey in his juvenile wailings and penchant for overstatement (Levy, 1985, p. 96). And much of Nietzsche's private correspondence does read like Morrissey's tear-stained and self-martyred 2013 *Autobiography*, it, too, being littered with italics and drenched in self-pity. Whereas Nietzsche wrote "Whenever I dip into my Zarathustra… I walk up and down my room for half-an-hour, unable to repress my sobs" (Brinton, 1948, p. 62), the former Smiths singer reminisces: "When my old friend Simon Topping [the frontman of Manchester band A Certain Ratio] appeared on the cover of the *NME*, I died a thousand deaths of sorrow and lay down in the woods to die" (Morrissey, 2013, p. 142).

In a letter dated January 2, 1874, Nietzsche continues in this vein: "Yesterday, the first day of the year, I looked into the future and trembled. Life is dreadful and hazardous — I envy anyone who is well and truly dead" (Hollingdale, 1985, p. 100). Yet even if Nietzsche was given to adolescent self-pity and self-obsession, his cries can't but help arouse sympathy in the reader, for Nietzsche's torments and unrelenting frustrations are evidently sincerely felt.

While Nietzsche the writer is thunderous and menacing, in person, however, he could be quite the reverse. One of his students at Basel recalled being "surprised by the modesty, even humility, of Nietzsche's demeanour" (Hollingdale, 1985, p. 53). Another contemporary thought Nietzsche had a "light laugh, a quiet way of speaking, and a cautious, pensive way of walking" (Soloman, 2003, p. 117). According to the French philosopher and poet Édouard Schuré (1841–1929), he was "timid, embarrassed and nearly always silent" in Wagner's presence (Hayman, 1980, p. 187). He was so afraid that Wagner would hate *Human, All Too Human*

(*Menschliches, Allzumenschliches*) that he toyed with the idea of publishing it under a pseudonym (Heller, 1988, p. 56).

On television documentaries, Nietzsche's voice as re-imagined by voice-over actors is invariably baritone or rasping and imposing—usually like Steven Berkoff in the 1983 James Bond film *Octopussy*. Yet Nietzsche spoke with a light, medium-high voice and in a Saxony accent, which other Germans mock on account of sounding slow and backwards, much as the English make fun of the Birmingham accent. He would have sounded less like Peter Cushing or Alan Rickman and more Jasper Carrot or Noddy Holder.

Nietzsche could be positively cheery in person. On one occasion, while travelling by train in Italy, Nietzsche and his sister got carried away exchanging German nonsense rhymes, so much so that the merriment caused an Englishman in the carriage to get up and leave, convinced was he that the pair were laughing at his expense. Copleston writes how "guests at the 'pension', where he was staying in the south of France, vied with one another to be next to him at table, as he was always the centre of a lively, cheerful and interesting conversation" (Copleston, 1975, p. 146). During one visit to Naples he spent a day at the residence of the German writer and enthusiast of the arts Malwida von Meysenbug, together with the writer Alfred Brenner and the philosopher Paul Rée, also a friend of Nietzsche's. Meysenbug recalled that "Nietzsche was indeed the soul of sweetness and kindliness! How well his good and amiable nature counterbalanced his destructive intelligence! How well he knew how to be gay, and to laugh with a good heart at the jokes which often came to disturb the serious atmosphere of our little circle" (Coplestone, 1975, p. 13). Meysenbug said that "I never saw him so lively. He laughed aloud from sheer joy" (letter from MvonM, 28/10/76, cited in de Botton, 2000, p. 209).

Perhaps his lighter side shouldn't surprise us. Those who are serious or gloomy by day sometimes have to be jovial or jaunty by night. Consider Mozart's scatological humour,

Charles Darwin's penchant for low-brow romance novels, or Sartre's fondness for the films of Charlie Chaplin and Buster Keaton, not to mention his impression of Donald Duck (Bakewell, 2016, p. 14). As Nietzsche put it himself: "Maturity consists in having rediscovered the seriousness one had as a child at play" (BGE 94).

So why was this preacher of harshness, this doomsayer, the man who epitomises silent loneliness, in person mild and polite and occasionally affable among his peers? How could a prophet of struggle appear so tender and be so lachrymose in his correspondence? Perhaps he recognised his own delicate temperament and sense of vulnerability, that he would have to face up to the fact that life is about struggle — or perish under its weight and woes. As Sigmund Freud's biographer, Ernest Jones, observed of Nietzsche: "he had more penetrating knowledge of himself than any man who ever lived or was likely to live" (Kaufmann, 1980, p. 49).

Apart from ill-health, Nietzsche had to contend with constant failure that only compounded the inherent feeling of worthlessness that he continually confessed to in his letters. As James Huneker wrote in 1909:

> The personal bias was inescapable, and this bias favoured sickness, not health. Hence his frantic sickness, not health. Hence his frantic apotheosis of health, the dance and laughter, and his admiration for Bizet's *Carmen*. Hence his constant employment of joyful imagery, of bold defiance to the sober workaday world. His famous injunction: "Be hard!" was meant for his own unhappy soul, ever nearing, like Pascal's, the abyss of black melancholy. (Huneker, 1909, p. 240)

In his lifetime, Nietzsche only achieved an inkling of the recognition he thought he deserved, and this was only in the final year of his sane life. Before that, all was disappointment. This is one reason for the increasingly combative and clamorous tone in his very last books. "For a long time, in fact for the greatest part of his active career, he was addressing a deaf world", one British author wrote in 1915.

"And who does not know how difficult it is to speak to the deaf in accents sweet and low? How many people, under such circumstances, do not succumb to the temptation to shout, to exaggerate their manner of speaking, and thereby also the matter of their speech?" (Wolf, 1923, p. 23).

Bertrand Russell dismissed such "power-phantasies of an invalid" (Russell, 1946, 1962, p. 734), but Nietzsche's ever more vociferous prose-style came not merely from the pen of a cripple but from someone for whom life had become relentless failure. "To lack not only health, but also money, recognition, love, and protection—and *not* to become a tragic grumbler: this constitutes the paradoxical character of our present condition, its *problem*", Nietzsche confessed to Gast in an 1888 letter from Nice. "As for myself, I have got into a state of *chronic vulnerability*, against which, when my condition is slightly improved, I take a sort of revenge which is not of the nicest description—that is to say, I adopt an attitude of excessive hardness" (Levy, p. 215).

He certainly needed to be hard. His 1881 book *Daybreak* (*Morgenröte*, sometimes translated as *Dawn*), according to the Nietzsche authority Michael Tanner, "was published early in July 1881, without creating any impression on the contemporary intellectual world whatever" (D vii). *Thus Spoke Zarathustra* also floundered. The first part was greeted with indifference by the German-speaking world. When in the spring of 1884 the second and third parts appeared in print, the response was so negligible that Nietzsche could find no publisher for the fourth part, so he published forty copies at his own expense. These were to be distributed to friends and acquaintances. He could only find seven people to send them to (Lavrin, 1971, p. 80). Although *Zarathustra* would become cult reading in the years immediately after his death, Nietzsche was resigned to the fact that everyone but himself regarded the work as "obscure, mysterious, and ridiculous" (Fuss & Shapiro, 1971, p. 82). *Zarathustra* suffered indignity from the start: its first part was held up at the printers in preference for a consignment of five hundred thousand hymn books, and then a cargo of anti-Semitic pamphlets (Lea, 1957, p. 289).

In 1886, only 114 copies of *Beyond Good and Evil* (*Jenseits von Gut und Böse*) were sold in the six months following its publication, also at the author's expense. By 1887 his career as a writer had actually cost him three thousand francs in printers' bills and earned him nothing in the way of royalties (Hayman, 1980, p. 312). The critics were just as unforgiving as the marketplace. *Beyond Good and Evil* was variously described as "eccentric", "pathological", "psychiatric", "diabolically calculating" and "higher nonsense" (Levy, 1985, p. 218; Hayman, 1980, p. 312). "What Nietzsche needs", exploded Rohde after having read *Beyond Good and Evil*, "is to get a proper job!" — a book he thought "paltry and almost childish" (Hollingdale, 1985, p. 43, p. 148).

Nietzsche, who boasted in print of being a loner and an outcast, nonetheless lamented in private correspondence his isolation and sense of rejection and failure. "How is it that no one feels insulted when I am abused?", he cried in February 1888. "And all these years no comfort, no drop of human sympathy, not a breath of love" (Levy, 1985, p. 218). He finally had to reassure himself with the resigned, prophetic words: "My time has not yet come, some are born post-humously" (EH WIWSCB.1).

Matters would never improve in his lifetime. He never forgave the Germans for not recognising his genius: "I have given the Germans the deepest books that they have ever possessed — a sufficient reason for their not having understood a word of them", he complained (TCOW, PS). His tirades against his fellow countrymen increased in frequency with each year of non-recognition. "How much dreary heaviness, lameness, dampness, sloppiness, how much *beer* there is in the German intellect! How can it possibly happen that young men who dedicate their existence to the most spiritual goals lack all sense of the first instinct of spirituality, *the spirit's instinct for self-preservation* — and drink beer?" (TOTI WTGL 2). Nietzsche's writings also caused great distress to his mother, a pious Christian, who read his books despite her son's exhortations not to. "Oh, Fritz, Fritz, if only you had kept to your Greeks!", she lamented (Copleston, 1975, p. 8).

Nietzsche's pugnacity and mania reached its apotheosis in his final work, *Ecce Homo*. Its infamous chapter titles, such as "Why I Am So Wise", "Why I Am So Clever", "Why I Write Such Excellent Books", have been deemed proof of his growing megalomania and impending insanity. The Italian philosopher Gianni Vattimo writes that *Ecce Homo*'s "messianic and exultant tones appear to herald the imminent onset of madness" (Vattimo, 1985, p. 88). Some have taken an alternative view. Nietzsche was playing a joke, mocking the genre of autobiography, daring to say in his which all authors do so implicitly in theirs. Nietzsche is merely being honest, "by simply saying what most authors don't *dare* to say, and in doing so both undermining the very pretentiousness of saying so and making a case for his own eccentric but now unified genius" (Soloman, 2003, p. 10; see also Tanner in EH Introduction, pp. 5–6).

The most likely cause for Nietzsche's final breakdown and madness was syphilis, contracted from a sole visit to a brothel as a young man. Others have suggested that the cause was dementia or brain cancer (S Tel 04/05/2003). Further speculation includes the suggestion that he was bipolar (see *Journal of the History of the Neurosciences*, 2013, 22 (2)), and that the recognition he began achieving in 1888 might have aroused an elation that actually tipped him over the precipice.

Published in 1886, *Beyond Good and Evil* (*Jenseits von Gut und Böse*), a plain-prose sequel to *Zarathustra* which attacks Christian morality as merely codified vested interests, was his first work to be received favourably. In a letter to Nietzsche in September 1886, the Renaissance historian Jacob Burckhardt remarked on "your astonishing survey of the whole area of current spiritual movements, and the power and art in your subtle delineation of details".

That same month the Bern newspaper *Der Bund* wrote of it: "Intellectual explosives, like the other kind, can be very useful... But it is well to put up a warning sign where they are being stored 'There is dynamite here'... Nietzsche is the first man who has found an escape route, but it is so terrifying that one feels genuinely frightened to see him treading this lonely, previously untrodden path" (Hayman, 1980, p. 300). On March 21, 1888, Nietzsche wrote of having "just been sent an intelligent and not unsympathetic notice" of *On The Genealogy of Morals* in the *National-Zeitung* from the reviewer himself, an assistant preacher at Bremen Cathedral. "Nietzsche is rude, but..." began the review's conclusion (Levy, 1985, p. 225).

The two most significant figures outside Germany to show an interest in Nietzsche were the French critic and historian, Hippolyte Tane, and the Dane, George Brandes, who in 1887 had written a book on Søren Kierkegaard. The next year Brandes delivered a series of lectures on Nietzsche at Copenhagen University, and wrote an admiring letter to the German. "You are one of the few men with whom I should like to speak", he said, praising Nietzsche's "aristocratic radicalism". This delighted Nietzsche, who replied, calling it "the shrewdest comment on me I have so far read". In his next letter, Brandes said "You are without doubt the most exciting of all German writers" (Copleston, 1975, p. 314).

When Nietzsche, now in Turin, received a letter from Brandes in April 1888 announcing the upcoming Nietzsche lectures in Copenhagen, "it was probably too late", as Copleston put it (Copleston, 1975, p. 25). Nietzsche was squandering his money, telling people that he was God. His landlady, alarmed by his midnight shrieking, was all set to evict him when on January 3 he had a mental collapse while watching a horse being whipped in the Piazza Carlo Alberto. He had rushed across the square, then wrapped his arms round it in a gesture of protection. It was a fitting end for a man who was known as the tough philosopher who deplored compassion, but in person was a tender, delicate soul.

In the ensuing days he sent a series of short letters to his friends, most of them signed "Dionysus". To Burckhardt, Nietzsche wrote: "last year I was crucified by the German doctors in a very drawn-out manner. Wilhelm, Bismarck, and all anti-Semites abolished" (Fuss & Shapiro, 1971, p. 144). To Gast, simply: "TO MY MAESTRO PIETRO, Sing me a new song; the world is transfigured; the Heavens are rejoicing. THE MAN ON THE CROSS" (Levy, 1985, p. 260). Elsewhere he ordered the German emperor to go to Rome to be shot and that other European powers take military action against Germany. Nietzsche never recovered. After being taken to a psychiatric clinic in Basel, he was moved to Jena. He was looked after first by his mother, and after her death in 1897, his sister, Elisabeth, who in 1885 had married Bernhard Förster, a German nationalist, anti-Semite and founder of the "Aryan settlement", Nueva Germania, in Paraguay.

Nietzsche never finished — or more likely abandoned — his project on "The Re-evaluation of All Values", but notes for it did appear posthumously in 1901 under the title *The Will to Power* (*Der Wille zur Macht*), a highly contentious book and unfortunately influential one. It was a collection of his notes in the mid-1880s, rather than a finished book. The original memos were far from his definitive thoughts. He hadn't published them either because he wasn't happy with them or they were unfinished. Among these sketches and works-in-progress is a shopping list — a reminder to buy toothpaste, buns and shoe polish (Bettany Hughes, BBC Arts website, 14/06/2016). The book bearing its name was assembled by his sister, who, acting as his curator, edited his manuscripts to fit into her and her husband's beliefs. Although much contained in *The Will to Power* is consistent with his writings in the mid-1880s, much of it was vague and, put in the wrong hands, politically dangerous. It was to become a foundational book for the Nazis.

Although Nietzsche never regained his mental faculties fully, he could still appreciate music and literature. In the first few years of indisposition, writes Copleston, "he impressed everyone by his patience, consideration and gentleness". When shown portraits of Wagner, he would say "I loved him". When his sister wept, as she sat by his side, he said: "Lisbeth, why do you cry? Are we not happy?" (Copleston, 1975, p. 27). His condition deteriorated following a stroke in 1898 and another the year following. He was weaker and talked with so much difficulty that he didn't want others to hear his voice. "I do not speak nicely", he said. But when he was given a new book, he said "Didn't I write good books too?" (Hayman, 1980, p. 349). After developing pneumonia, he died at about noon on August 25, 1900. At his funeral at the church of Röcken bei Lützen, Peter Gast gave his funeral oration, proclaiming: "Holy be your name to all future generations!"

By this time, the cult of Nietzsche had begun to sweep Europe. His publishers, fully aware as to the potential allure of the "dangerous, mad philosopher", eagerly promoted his books in the 1890s, while, at the behest of his sister, Nietzsche the mental invalid became an exhibition figure in Weimer for his growing band of admirers. As early as 1893, one French critic noted: "No matter what critical review one thumbs, one finds Nietzsche's name in the table of contents… Every day the army of his disciples and imitators increases" (Brinton, 1948, pp. 178–79).

He appealed initially to *fin de siècle* Romantics and decadents who liked to believe Nietzsche had gone insane after having fully apprehended humanity's ghastly fate, to having perceived some horrible, elusive truth. A later devotee, Ernst Bertram, called Nietzsche's insanity a "proud transition" and an "ascent into the mystic" (Hollingdale, 1985, p. 177). For German Expressionists, who had a fascination with madness and its supposed liberating qualities, Nietzsche became "both a spokesman and an exemplar" (Watson, 2016, p. 35). He became a tragic martyr, and his madness adjudged to be the seal of his genius. The esoteric Austrian philosopher Rudolf Steiner remarked of his visits to Naumburg to pay homage to Nietzsche, where "he sat enthroned on the veranda above in solemn awfulness, unconcerned with us, like a god of Epicurus" (Hollingdale, 1985, p. 177).

Nietzsche's detractors, especially Christians, saw his madness as proof of the perils of atheism. Nietzsche's own philosophy had driven him insane, they said. Romantics and German nationalists were both keen to dismiss the theory of syphilis, this being such a squalid disease for a "Superman", while critics and devotees were keen, for opposite reasons, to play up its psychological cause—diabolic insanity or mystical flight into another world. Anthony Ludovici had a more prosaic explanation: "Nietzsche's madness proves little, except that solitude, poverty, disappointment and over-work can finally overcome a very fine brain" (Ludovici, 1927, p. viii).

His madness was central to his cult, nonetheless, and his reputation spread throughout all sections of society. By the turn of the century various groups in Europe were starting to call themselves Nietzscheans: artisans in the spirit of William Morris who were repelled by industrialism and conformity; radical Bohemians who saw in his anti-bourgeois individualism the spirit of Oscar Wilde; Prussian aristocrats who were foes of democracy; anarchists drawn to his energetic spirit and violent language. The French critic and thinker Charles Andler claimed him as a socialist, writing in his *Nietzsche, sa vie et sa pensée* that, "one may legitimately call the system of Nietzsche a socialism", in that the master's writings supported "a European working-class which would be a class of masters" (Brinton, 1948, p. 180). For decadents, "beyond good and evil" was a green light to libertinism. His "will to power" appealed to angry radical types who wanted to lob a bomb at a politician, or a politician who sought to expand his country's frontiers.

In his 1908 polemic, *The Nietzsche Cult: A Chapter in the History of Aberrations of the Human Spirit*, the philosopher

Wolfgang Beckers noted that the young seemed drawn to him on account of his writings being "deep". Yet at the same time German colonial officials in Africa were likewise impressed by Nietzsche's spirit of nobility and higher beings, feeling "it was suited perfectly to 'the colonial mode of rule'" (Brinton, 1948, p. 37). His anti-Christianity was understood to endorse atheism and he was soon recruited by those preaching sexual liberation. Havelock Ellis, co-author of *Sexual Inversion* (1897), the first English language textbook on homosexuality, commended Nietzsche for his determined effort to "destroy modern morals", hailing him as the "greatest spiritual force" since Goethe (Himmelfarb, 1995, p. 189).

In his 1909 study *The Quintessence of Nietzsche*, an early British champion of his work, J.M. Kennedy, noted that "nothing is commoner than to hear the view expressed that Nietzsche was an anarchist of anarchists: a man who desired to upset all hitherto established law and order, not only in politics and the ordinary relations between man and a man… Hence hundred of Socialists, all of whom Nietzsche would have held in contempt, boldly proclaimed themselves his followers" (Kennedy, 1909, p. 53). Indeed, some perceived and praised Nietzsche as the arch-nemesis of socialism. Upon the publication of the first English edition of *Thus Spoke Zarathustra* in English in 1896, *The Times*, praising "the peculiar beauty of Nietzsche's style, even in the form of translation", welcomed him as the "champion of individualism against the invading doctrines of the Socialist". (In Britain, the *National Observer* was less enthusiastic about the book: "a more extremely absurd, and at the same time pretentious and offensive volume it has never been our lot to meet" —Thatcher, 1970, p. 31.) Nietzsche was now the all-weather, all-purpose rebel. "'Every idiot fancies himself an *Übermensch*' was a remark made once to me by an erudite Bavarian", reflected the Anglican priest and philosopher John Neville Figgis in his 1917 study *The Will to Freedom, or*

The Gospel of Nietzsche and the Gospel of Christ (Figgis, 1917, p. 214).

Nietzsche, so painfully neglected by his countrymen during his life and sanity, was now embraced with gusto in Germany. In the country, there emerged at the turn of the century a Youth Movement, which rebelled against the perceived patriotism, philistinism and materialism of the Kaiser-reich. To them, as Nietzsche had foreseen, "Germany had been able to become strong only by ceasing to be Germany" (Wohl, 1980, p. 47), as industrialisation and modernity replaced the Germany of peaceful hamlets. This movement sought cultural re-purification, and it was in this spirit that *Thus Spoke Zarathustra* became cult reading. Nietzsche evenings became commonplace, consisting of social gatherings accompanied by music and recitals of his texts (Watson, 2014, 1948, p. 33). Richard Strauss's tone poem *Also Sprach Zarathustra* premiered in Frankfurt-am-Main in November 1896, while Mahler's Third Symphony had originally been entitled *The Gay Science* (Watson, p. 35).

As Robert Wohl writes in *The Generation of 1914* (1980), the quest for "purification" became more extreme as the new century unfolded. "War was the seedbed of culture, the foundation of morality, and the form of social intercourse that brought men closest together. Peace came at a cultural price too high to pay. This was the message that many people derived from Nietzsche's teachings" (Wohl, p. 213). Writing on the origins of the First World War, the historian James Joll observed that by the turn of the century "he was already a figure of European importance whose teachings were being quoted, misquoted and interpreted in a number of different ways, and in the years before 1914 no one with any intellectual pretensions was ignorant of his work" (Joll, in Koch, 1982, p. 323). Nietzsche became a figurehead for a young restless generation that felt alienated by comfortable, safe Edwardian life. Joll writes how Nietzsche's writings, often misunderstood, taken out of context or perverted, "contributed to the acceptance of the idea of war not just as lamentable episode in international relations but as an experience desirable and salutary in itself" (Joll, in Kohl, 1982, p. 323).

When hostilities came in 1914, the people of Europe literally took to the streets to rejoice. Today, we are often prone to accept the Poets Narrative of the First World War, that it was the result of terrible diplomatic blundering, of warmongering governments, and that it was the ordinary men, the lions lead by donkeys, who were its victims. Yet there was also a palpable appetite for war among the young men of Europe, a generation that had becoming fascinated by the idea of sacrifice and bloodshed, a mood epitomised by the words of the 1916 Irish revolutionary, Pádraig Pearse, that "blood is a cleansing and sanctifying thing". Nietzsche had especially galvanised the Young Serb movement, and Gavril Princip, the assassin of Franz Ferdinand, was fond of reciting *Ecce Homo*, with the line "Insatiable as flame, I burn and consume myself" (Joll, in Koch, 1982, p. 324). For the generation that sought blood, sacrifice and purification, Nietzsche had been their prophet.

In his *Quintessence of Nietzsche* Kennedy had already warned: "Nietzsche is a dangerous weapon to be handled by those not accustomed to fight intellectual battles, and one must beware of him in an age when the land is suffering from nervous breakdown, when rumours of air-ships sailing for unknown destinations send tremors of fear through the once stolid John Bull, when wails and gnashing of teeth arise from all and sundry as the Kaiser reviews his troops" (Kennedy, 1909, p. x). The First World War pushed sales of *Thus Spoke Zarathustra* to new highs, both in Britain and America and in Germany, where it became a "must" for the soldier's knapsack (Kaufmann, 1974, p. 8), and 140,000 copies of the book were sold in 1917 alone (Joll, in Kohl, 1982, p. 323).

In his 1915 edition of *The Philosophy of Nietzsche*, A. Wolf observed: "Since the outbreak of war Nietzsche has acquired unenviable notoriety. His name has become a byword among us. Thanks to the influence of the Press and the pulpit he is commonly regarded as one of the villains in the terrible drama that is now claiming nearly all the world a stage" (Wolf, 1923, p. 9). An enterprising bookseller in London's Strand even christened it the "Euro-Nietzschean" war (Wolf, 1923, p. 10). As Walter Kaufmann writes, among the Allied countries: "Nietzsche began to be considered the apostle of German ruthlessness and barbarism." His "Superman" began to be associated with the German nation, and its militarism and imperialism were read into Nietzsche's concept of power. This was a gross distortion, insisted Wolf. "Teutomania… was very far from Nietzsche's heart and soul. It is the Prussian jingo's heart wrapped in Nietzsche's skin" (Wolf, 1923, p. 18).

When peace came in 1918, the first part of Europe's great conflagration was over, but it had not extinguished the warlike spirit of the new century, in which fascism and communism — new atheistic man-made, power-worshipping moralities — emerged to fill the nihilist void that Nietzsche had predicted. Germany's humiliation and the economic crash of the 1930s ensured the second instalment would take place. Benito Mussolini was an eager Nietzsche reader, and his fascist slogan *"Guerra, sola igiene del mondo"* ("War, only hygiene of the world") had a decidedly Nietzschean ring (Joll, in Kohl, 1982, p. 325).

Adolf Hitler was also typical of his generation, in being keen for the Great War and brutalised by it as a consequence. He professed to be an admirer of Nietzsche, but he professed to admire a lot of thinkers and he was a very superficial reader of them all. For instance, one of Nietzsche's constant topics, which he returns to repeatedly, is his loathing of anti-Semites. He may not have liked Judaism as a religion, not least because it begat Christianity, but he admired Jews and had contempt for their detractors. As a section of *The Will to Power* explains: "What a blessing a Jew is among Germans! See the obtuseness, the flaxen head, the blue eyes, and the lack of intellect in the face, the language, and the bearing; the lazy habit of stretching the limbs and the need of repose among Germans—a need which is not the result of overwork, but of the disgusting excitation and over-excitation caused by alcohol" (WTP 45).

Still, Hitler would have been vulnerable to Nietzsche's more wild and excessive assertions plucked from in *The Will to Power* by fascist propagandists. There was much here that taken out of context easily suited Nazi ideology. "Life is a result of war, society is a means to war", Nietzsche writes (53), condemning "the degenerate" and "decadence" (56), praising man's "warlike virtue" (125). He wrote of the Jews and their "an instinctive ability to create an advantage, a means of seduction out of every superstitious supposition" (199). Careless talk costs lives, as they say, even if Nietzsche's sister is blamed for the final content of *The Will to Power* and its most inflammatory sections.

"Such rantings from one of Germany's most original minds must have struck a responsive chord in Hitler's littered mind. At any rate he appropriated them for his own —not only the thoughts but the philosopher's penchant for grotesque exaggeration, and often his very words", writes William Shirer in *The Rise and Fall of the Third Reich*. "That in the end Hitler considered himself the superman of Nietzsche's prophecy can not be doubted" (Shirer, 1960, p. 101). German restlessness and activism was blamed on his *Will to Power*, and Nazism too, with its satanic rhetoric of *Untermensch*, by implication linked to Nietzsche's counterpart, the *Übermensch*. "I play with a burden that would crush every other mortal", Nietzsche had written from Turin to his sister in December 1888. "However the judgement may fall, for or against me, my name is in any case linked up with a fatality the magnitude of which is unutterable" (Levy, 1985, p. 254).

It was the philosopher and translator Walter Kaufmann who began the lengthy rehabilitation of Nietzsche, with his landmark work of 1950 *Nietzsche: Philosopher, Psychologist, Antichrist*, which went into four editions and remains in print to this day. Reflecting on this process in the 1974 edition, Kaufmann remembered the mood in "Anglo-Saxon countries where the war-begotten misconceptions have never been eradicated from the popular mind. The advent of Hitler and the Nazis' brazen adaptation of Nietzsche have strengthened these misapprehensions" (Kaufmann, 1974, p. 9). Arthur Danto's best-selling *Nietzsche as Philosopher* (1965) aided in the restoration, later, as did Michel Foucault's writing on power and knowledge in the 1960s and 1970s. Foucault especially focused on Nietzsche's belief that "truth" stems from the desire for power and has no eternal objective foundation. Nietzsche's dissecting of Western morality in *On the Genealogy of Morals* also became a point of reference for Jacques Derrida and his theory of "deconstruction".

Nietzsche became the godfather of the mood of spirit of postmodernism emergent after 1968, the year that in Paris and Prague witnessed the end of the socialist dream. The shortcomings, and then failure, of the socialist experiments in the late 20th century lead to a realignment within the Left-wing intelligentsia. The Left began its retreat from optimistic, Marxist-teaching which believed in progress and rationality, and there ensued a flight towards postmodernism, with its emphasis on personal subjectivity, localised knowledge and "truth" being a mask for power.

The Left no longer talks of progress, rights, solidarity and equality, but "respecting identities", "self-affirmation", subjective experience and personal "choice". The personal has gradually become the political. Since the 1960s, notes the conservative philosopher Roger Scruton, Nietzsche's "beliefs and attitudes, have endeared him to radical critics of Western society, and caused him to be conscripted to secular causes — feminism, socialism, egalitarianism, 'multiculturalism' — which he himself would have greeted with cavernous laughter" (Scruton, 2002, p. 199).

Western society in the past fifty years has gradually moved away from ideas of collectivity. The appeals of nation, religion, family class and other wider collective identities have gradually withered. The cult of Nietzsche on the ascent in the 1960s owes principally to the growth in individualism. The primacy of "the self" above universal ideals first came to the fore in the 1960s in the social sphere, and then in the 1980s in the economic sphere. Personal "choice" is now paramount; subjective experience triumphs objective investigation. The diminishing of traditional affinity to political parties and the growth of "anti-Establishment" populism in the 21st century has taken place in a new digital age in which lived experience is tailored towards the self. Nietzsche fits ideally into a culture that no longer believes in Left or Right, which no longer believes in loyalty to that which is beyond the individual.

Once more Nietzsche has become the one-size fits all rebel. Quoting Nietzsche has become a favourite method of proving we are strong and unafraid. "Look at me!", it screams. Yet to quote Nietzsche en masse is itself a narcissistic, herd-like act, which he would find risible. When everyone's a rebel, no one is. This is why, even when we venerate his very name, we become herd thinkers. And Nietzsche would not only urge us to get over ourselves, he would ask that we get over him. In order to reject him, however, we must first embrace him.

1

The Superman
Identity politics

Ours is an age of so-called "identity politics", where people's identity is "celebrated" and must be "respected". We see this manifest in modern feminism with the exhortation that "the personal is the political". Race and identity remain at the forefront of discourse in American culture and politics, as the campaign slogan "Black Lives Matter" demonstrates. We witness it in disputes about the rights of the transgendered to identify themselves according to as they wish, and debates over the nomenclature surrounding "gender fluid" people. On Facebook today, you can choose from innumerable different gender categories. Parents now fret if their ten-year-old "identifies as gender non-binary" or not.

The politics of identity have been central to British political discourse for some decades, in terms of the emergence of Scottish nationalism, in our relationship with the rest of Europe and in debates that surround immigration, multiculturalism and integration. "What does it mean to be British" is a question perpetually asked. On government forms we are asked to tick boxes of identity according to ethnicity, gender and religion.

Today, one of the worst things you can do, especially among student and Left-wing circles, is question a person's "sense of self" or their very "personhood". "I do not believe that students should be required to listen to their own rights and personhood debated", as one University of North

Colorado student recently complained, complaining about a lecture on transgenderism in which, as the *Washington Examiner* put it, those attending were "forced to hear opposing viewpoints" (*Washington Examiner* 22/06/16).

Identity politics are often presented as a progressive and liberating, emancipatory pursuit. For feminists since Simone De Bouvoir it's a matter concerned with wrestling back from society how women are defined in order that they can define themselves. For transsexuals it's about "being true to oneself". People who seek to change their gender often complain that they are "trapped" in the wrong body. For gay people it is concerned with recognition and being free from persecution. Some say they want to become "who they really are" and not to be defined either by biology or how society seeks to categorise them.

Religious identities must also be recognised and religious beliefs respected on account of being "sincerely-held". Hence the half-jokey move to have the Jedi religion classed as a legitimate faith on census forms, or for more serious initiatives by humanists and atheists to have their belief – or lack of it – officially sanctioned. The humanist writer A.C. Grayling in 2011 even published an atheists' bible, *The Good Book*, and the following year his fellow philosopher Alain de Botton called for the creation of a "temple to atheism" in central London (*Guardian* 26/01/12).

Identity politics is regarded as self-empowerment. To create oneself as one wishes, to be whoever one wishes, is seen as a noble pursuit. To declare one's identity in public is seen as a human right and even an obligation. Identity is regarded as essential today – essential in both definitions of the word. It is viewed as the quality that determines existence, and also something that is very, very important.

Nietzsche would laugh at identity politics, or the very notion that people have or even want to anchor themselves to a fixed identity. Labels only imprison us. For Nietzsche, life was concerned with forever becoming, for striving to go beyond oneself, to break free from confines: "Speak not of gifts, or innate talents! One can name all kinds of great men who were not very gifted. But they acquired greatness, became 'geniuses' (as we say)" (HATH 163). This is why Nietzsche's thought was essentially incompatible with Nazism, with its notion that races and identities had essences and could be thus classified. As he wrote on 1885: "I've as yet managed to mount little enthusiasm for 'the Germanic essence', and even less for keeping this 'glorious' race pure. On the contrary, on the contrary…" (Fuss & Shapiro, 1971, p. 86). To adhere to any label is to cage yourself within one.

He outlined his philosophy of overcoming most vividly in *Thus Spoke Zarathustra*, which introduces The Superman, the individual who goes beyond. "I teach you the Superman. Man is something that should be overcome", said Zarathustra. "Man is a rope, fastened between animal and Superman—a rope over an abyss. A dangerous going-across, a dangerous wayfaring, a dangerous looking-back, a dangerous shuddering and staying-still. What is great in man is that he is a bridge and not a goal" (TSZ PROL.3, 4). The Superman is not a biological or Darwinian concept, rather he represents a state of mind, an ideal of perpetual self-betterment through ceaseless exertion. Contrary to Darwin, life for Nietzsche "is not a question of the species but of the individuals… Life is not the adaptation of inner circumstances to outer ones, but will to power, which, working from within, incorporates and subdues more and more of that which is 'outside'" (WTP 681). Nietzsche's Superman breaks constraints and superpasses ideology, going beyond the herd and himself.

The modern-day philosopher John Gray calls the Superman "a ridiculous figure" (Gray, 2005, p. 48), and it can be hard sometimes to take the word seriously on account of its association with the comic-book super-hero. The English word was an invention of George Bernard Shaw's, his translation of the German *Übermensch*, which has occasionally been rendered also as "Over-man" or "Beyond-man".

Since English has no one word that corresponds to *über*, which can mean "above", "over", "across" and "beyond", some purists prefer to leave it in the German. To the average English monoglot, however, *Übermensch* looks superficially too much like *Untermensch*, with all its negative connotations. So, for brevity's sake, Superman will do here, its association with the comic character notwithstanding.

In his account of the Superman, Nietzsche was stressing the imperative not to be comfortable and complacent in who we are, but to perpetually strive in a process of self-overcoming. As Arthur C. Danto put it: "Nietzsche was *not* asking for a release from its cage of the beast which morality hemmed in; he was not, in the name of some specious theory of happy savagehood, urging reversion to barbarity, or to an infantile immediacy in the reduction of drives. Nietzsche was asking that we go *beyond* what we are not *back* to what we were" (Danto, 1970, p. 180, original italics). The Superman is never content in who he or she is, only in what he or she can be, in how to be a better, stronger, higher version of themselves.

Nietzsche believed the "I" and the fixed self was a fiction. "Our 'ego' — which is *not* one with the unitary controlling force of our beings! — is really only an imagined synthesis: therefore there can *be* no '*egotistical*' actions" (cited in Levy, 1985, p. 295). Rather than a unitary "I", we are a collection of our drives, passions, appetites and memories, which in turn are created within a particular society, within a certain language. For Nietzsche, talking of "becoming who I really am" would sound the highest nonsense. There is no transcendental "self" to be true to.

For Nietzsche, we cannot be "true to ourselves" because we are guided by an assemblage of irrational forces, what he called it the Will to Power, and thus always in flux. This Will to Power comprises such forces as hunger, sexual desire, impulses, dreams and thoughts that come to us of their own volition. "A thought comes when it will, not when 'I' will", he wrote in *Beyond Good and Evil* (BGE 17). His "Will to

Power" doesn't just mean "the desire for power", although it can degenerate into that. Nietzsche believed that power was the guiding force in the universe, and that it is up to us to master it and use it to our advantage. Nietzsche saw life as the need to harness, dominate and control both the external forces that operate on oneself and the internal forces within us.

We are shaped, too, by history and the environment into which we are born. "Our own opinions. The first opinion that occurs to us when we are suddenly asked about a matter is usually not our own, but only the customary one, appropriate to our caste, position, or parentage; our own opinions seldom swim near the surface", he wrote in *Human, All Too Human* (HATH 571). We think in a language not of our making (I didn't invent these words of English in which I write and which you now read), and this language shapes our thoughts and our reality, and also gives us the illusion of perfect autonomy. "One believed in the soul as one believed in grammar and the grammatical subject. We used to say that 'I' is the condition, 'think' the predicate which con-ditions — thinking being an activity for which a subject, as cause, must be thought", he wrote in *Beyond Good and Evil* (BGE 54).

Yet while Nietzsche believed "the self" a myth, he still hailed the agency of the individual. One can be consumed by the Will to Power and become envious and resentful, to use this power for ill, or — not unlike the Force from the "Star Wars" films — one can harness its powers to become a noble, life-affirming Superman: "Shrewdness, clarity, severity and logicality as weapons against the ferocity of the drives" (WTP 433), he exhorted. Central in doing so is looking out-side and beyond oneself. While we can be slaves to our passions, we can also be masters of them. (The Monty Python sketch got it wrong. Nietzsche didn't believe in free will as a governing force; our instincts are too powerful for that (EH WIAD.8). But he did believe these instincts could be mastered and directed.)

The greatest impediment to becoming a great person, something bigger, is to dwell on oneself, on who one is. "Acknowledge yourself", he wrote in 1868, "through action, not observation" (cited in Hayman, 1980, p. 103). As Nike say: Just Do It. For Nietzsche, the self is a vortex forever in flux, and we should channel that energy to create ourselves anew: "first one needs to emancipate oneself from one's chains, and finally one must emancipate oneself from this emancipation. Each of us, even if in very different ways, has to toil against the chain-sickness, even after he has smashed the chains" (letter to Lou Salomé, cited in Cate, 2002, p. 371).

Nietzsche thus thought that introspection, going back inside oneself, was pointless and harmful. "But how can we find ourselves again, and how can man know himself? He is a thing dark and veiled", Nietzsche wrote in 1874: "it is a painful and dangerous undertaking thus to tunnel into oneself and to force one's way down into the shaft of one's being by the nearest path. A man who does it can easily so hurt himself that no physician can cure him" (UM 4 i). He urged us not to know ourselves, but strive beyond ourselves. "The precondition for becoming what one is is not to have the least notion of what one is" (EH WIASOC).

Life is about doing, not being. As Zarathustra said: "You say 'I' and are proud of this word. But greater than this — and which you do not want to believe in — is your body and its great intelligence: this does not say 'I' but performs 'I'" (TSZ ODB). One explores, makes mistakes, falls at fences. Nietzsche hailed "the temporary sidepaths and wrong turnings, the delays, the 'modesties', the serious squandered on tasks, which lie outside *the* task — have their own meaning and value. They are an expression of a great sagacity, even the supreme sagacity: where *nosce te ipsum* [know thyself] would be the recipe for destruction, self-forgetfulness, self-*misunderstanding*, self-diminution, -narrowing, -mediocratizing" (EH WIASC.9).

The idea that someone's identity is something to be attained and retained, let alone to be "respected", would be laughable. To "know oneself" is to stay still, to become stale. Nietzsche, as the American scholar Crane Brinton put it in his 1941 study, "hates anything finished, complete, contented" (Brinton, 1948, p. 108). This is why today's proponents of "respecting people's identity" are so conservative, the very antithesis to Nietzsche's revolutionary spirit. Although many "trans" people object to the idea of gender being a public, performative act based on gender stereotype, there are some who interpret gender politics today along conservative lines.

Consider the way Bruce Jenner was celebrated on the front cover of *Vanity Fair* in July 2015, appearing here as Caitlyn Jenner to worldwide acclaim. For some, it seemed, "becoming a woman" now means having one's penis removed, putting on lipstick and high-heel shoes. That is praised as a "brave" and challenging thing, when it is a conservative, retrogressive, gender-stereotypical act. As the novelist Lionel Shriver wrote recently: "We have entered instead an oppressively gendered world, in which identity is more bound up in one's sex than ever before... The women's liberation movement of my adolescence advocated a release from gender roles, and now we are entrenching them — pigeonholing ourselves with picayune precision on a continuum of gender identity, as if arriving at the right relationship to cliché is tantamount to self-knowledge" (*Prospect*, 21/04/16).

Nietzsche warned against: "the vanity of making one's own personality the centre of interest" (WTP 97). Once introspection becomes fetishised and identity sanctified, narcissism follows. This manifests itself today not merely in selfies, the need for people to "like" your photos on Facebook, but student union politics, that which seeks "safe spaces" to protect people with their brittle selves, or bans speakers with "offensive" views. Nietzsche would bristle at today's culture of narcissism, the need for your identity to be "respected" or "affirmed" and your need to be "liked".

Identity politics, and the need to be respected, fosters passive dependency on the opinions of others. To choose one of Facebook's 59 gender categories is to define oneself by labels designated by others. The very act of assigning oneself an identity in the public sphere is itself needy, an abrogation of your own will and independence, a capitulation to the unseen power of others. As he wrote in *Human, All To Human*: "So long as you go on being praised, you must believe that you are not yet on your own course, but on someone else's" (HATH II 240). He would ask parents not to worry what gender their ten-year-old belonged to — he would let the child be. The transgendered Nietzschean would reject all gender labels. He or she wouldn't give a damn what your boss called you.

Nietzsche would have recognised how the politics of identity inevitably leads to self-obsession and self-aggrandisement, and from there to belligerence and intolerance. It's no coincidence that today's age of the politics of identity is the same age of selfies on Instagram and student intolerance towards people who have the temerity to "question their sense of self". Nietzsche had little time for "those loafers who look a mere three or four steps ahead and are almost content to burrow inside themselves. We psychologists of the future — we have little patience with introspection: we almost take it for a sign of degeneration when an instrument tries 'to know itself'" (WTP 426).

A free spirit would not "be true to himself", but rebel against himself. Nietzsche extolled "war against oneself, that is to say self-control, self-outwitting" (BGE 200). Only when an individual has freed themselves from all constraints, all categories and all ideologies will he or she be a free spirit.

2

What doesn't kill you makes you stronger
Therapy culture

The idea that people shouldn't be offended or have their feelings hurt is allied to the notion that happiness and contentment should be the norm and life's ultimate goal. If we are unhappy, we are lead to understand that there is something "wrong" with us, or that perhaps we even have a medical or psychiatric "condition". There are forever headlines about growing levels of "stress, anxiety and depression" in our society, states of mind that are increasingly placed under the category "mental health issues". In the 20th century an entire psychiatric industry was built on the premise that bad thoughts were abnormal, and by the 21st century the pharmaceutical industry with its "happy pills" has made the happiness industry its own.

For Nietzsche, life was not about happiness. For him life was foremost struggle. If anything, happiness is a consequence of struggle, but certainly not an aim. "The right way of life does not want happiness, turns away from happiness" (WTP 437). It shouldn't be the norm. And since the turn of the millennium, Nietzsche's idea that life is about struggle and overcoming failures has taken root in niche areas in the boardroom and in the self-help book market. *Success through Failure* and *Why Success Always Starts with Failure* are the titles of two popular books of recent years. "Stress is a kind of energy that we can harness", exhorts the Nietzschean author Ian Robertson (*Sunday Telegraph* 16/06/16). People now even talk about their "greatest failures".

Yet despite these advances in some walks of life, we still talk mostly in mainstream society of "anxiety" and "depression" as if they are bad for us, that they should be eradicated. Nietzsche, contrarily, prescribed adversarial feeling as being good for us: "Man, the boldest animal and the one most accustomed to pain, does *not* repudiate suffering as such; he *desires* it, he even seeks it out" (GOM 3.28). Nietzsche asserted that "If we possess our *why* of life we can put up with almost any *how*" (TOTI MAA 12). The Nietzschean sounding quote, "To live is to suffer, to survive is to find some meaning in the suffering", is often now heard in rehabilitation institutions or organisations helping people with addictions. (This quote, commonly misattributed to Nietzsche himself, actually comes from Gordon W. Allport in the preface of the 1959 English translation of *Man's Search for Meaning*, by the late Austrian neurologist and psychiatrist Viktor Frankl, a devotee of Nietzsche who said "If there is meaning in life at all, then there must be meaning in suffering" (Frankl, 1959, p. 9).) Nietzsche taught us to embrace adversity and hardship in order to overcome them.

Nietzsche had been impressed by Schopenhauer's vision of mankind without ultimate purpose and life without meaning, a vision of existence characterised by frustration and suffering. Schopenhauer wrote that "misfortune in general is the rule", and that "happiness and satisfaction are *negative* in their nature; in other words, they are merely freedom from suffering; whilst pain is the positive element of existence" (Schopenhauer, 1962, p. 85, 26). Schopenhauer maintained that happiness is but a diminution of pain and only by negating life could man be happy. Calm and serenity are achieved by escape. Yet whereas Schopenhauer held that in life one must escape from one's suffering, Nietzsche held that we must confront it. While Schopenhauer's ideal man masters life through denial, asceticism, resignation and renunciation, Nietzsche's Superman does so by affirmation and confrontation, by swallowing up adversity and spitting it out again.

In *Daybreak* (1881) Nietzsche outlines his ideal man who extolled human suffering to achieve greatness. "He thinks with contempt of the warm, comfortable misty world in which the healthy man wanders... he takes pleasure in conjuring up this contempt as though out of the deepest depths of Hell and thus subjecting his soul to the bitterest pain... Raise yourself above your life as above your suffering, look down into the deep and the unfathomable depths!" (D 114). Such an acceptance of the forces of suffering was the handmaiden of creation. The genius is he or she who creatively embraces adversity.

Nietzsche spoke of that "discipline of suffering, of *great* suffering... in undergoing, enduring, interpreting, exploiting misfortune" (BGE 155), and that "all events, all motion, all becoming, as a determination of degrees and relations to force, as *struggle*" (WTP 552). Happiness ultimately results after one has embraced a difficult task and then defeated it. "Pleasure and displeasure are mere consequences... every victory, every feeling of pleasure, every event, presupposes a resistance overcome" (WTP 702). One embraces unhappiness to achieve its opposite effect. Addressing "comfortable... people", Nietzsche said that "happiness and unhappiness are sisters and even twins that either grow up together or, as in your case, remain small together" (TJS 338).

For Nietzsche, contentment as a mere primary goal was on a par with Aldous Huxley's "soma" from *Brave New World*, that drug which stultifies and erases all worries. "The illusion which makes people happy is more harmful than the illusion which is immediately followed by evil results: the latter increases keenness and mistrust, and purifies the understanding; the former merely narcoticises" (WTP 453).

Happiness as a commodity to be sought is a drug, and dangerous for that. "Fine feelings and noble impulses ought, speaking physiologically, to be classified with the narcotics: their abuse is followed by precisely the same results as the abuse of any other opiate — *weak nerves*" (WTP 453). Being unhappy is intrinsic to the human experience because it stimulates struggle. "All this is diametrically opposed to 'happiness' as understood on the level of the powerless, the oppressed, of those who suppurate with poisonous and hostile feelings, those for whom happiness appears as narcotic, anaesthetic, calm, peace" (GOM 1.20).

Nietzsche's idea of life being struggle was intimately associated with his *Übermensch*, the warrior in spirit who has contempt for comfort and who decries safety and contentment. In their call to do away with unhappiness, Christians, democrats, humanitarians and utilitarians unwisely diminished the role of suffering. "To regard *states of distress* in general as an objection, as something that must be *abolished*, is the *niaiserie* [foolishness] *par excellence*... almost as stupid as would be the will to abolish the bad weather" (EH WIAD.4). It was suffering that awakened our spirits, arousing inner resistance to it. He spoke not of reducing suffering but of transforming it into a creative force through self-discipline.

Achievement demands pain and suffering, failure and setback. To climb the highest mountain or to fly to the Moon requires both the acceptance of pain and the fortitude to overcome this to achieve one's goals. As John F. Kennedy put it: "We choose to go to the Moon in this decade and do the other things, not because they are easy, but because they are hard." Suffering is thus intrinsic to fulfilment, as any mountain climber or Olympic gold medal athlete will relate. Life involves failures and setbacks, as winners of television talent shows bear witness, what with their tears of joy and tales of long "emotional rollercoasters". As Nietzsche elaborated in *Human, All Too Human*: "You find the burden of life too heavy? Then you must increase the burden of your life. If the sufferer is finally longing to drink from the River Lethe, he must become a hero to be certain of finding it" (HATH II 401).

As was his habit, Nietzsche employs natural imagery to serve as a metaphor. In *The Joyous Science* (*Die fröhliche Wissenschaft*, sometimes translated as *The Joyous Wisdom* or *The Gay Science* — the former title using an inaccurate translation of *Wissenschaft*, the latter using an almost now redundant use of the English word "gay"), he asked us to examine the lives of the best and most fruitful people, and then consider "whether a tree that is supposed to grow to a proud height can dispense with bad weather and storms". He saw forces beyond our rational control in a similar light, that we too must suffer and endure hatred, jealousy, mistrust, avarice and hardness if we are to become great. "The poison of which weaker natures perish strengthens the strong" (TJS 19).

He returned to the sentiment that hardship builds character in *Twilight of the Idols* (1888) with the better known maxim "What does not kill me, makes me stronger". This maxim can be found in much corporate motivational and self-help material these days. The 1982 film *Conan the Barbarian* begins with it, and it's been used by the singers Kanye West, Kelly Clarkson and Marilyn Manson. It's also a favourite quote of Mark Lawrenson, the BBC television football pundit, even though, taken literally, it evidently isn't true. As one letter in *Viz* comic in April 2016 pointed out: "They say 'what doesn't kill you makes you stronger'. Try telling that to my cousin. He was a champion weight lifter until he got hit by a BT van. Now he drinks his food through a straw."

As Camus wrote in *The Rebel*, his long 1951 essay on revolutionary thought: "Because his mind was free, Nietzsche knew that freedom of the mind is not a comfort, but an achievement that one aspires to and obtains, at long last, after an exhausting struggle" (Camus, 2000, p. 44). And if suffering was intrinsic to achievement then happiness could prove detrimental to us. There must be no room for complacency in triumph, Nietzsche said, as "a great victory is a great danger. Human nature bears a triumph less easily than a defeat" (UM 1 i).

When Nietzsche invokes the need for cruelty, struggle and harshness, he is referring to life's personal contests and exertions and the need to be strong in the face of adversity. His *Übermensch* bore no relation to the Nazi Brownshirt thug or sadistic SS guard whose sadism was directed against others. Nietzsche asks that pain and harshness be directed towards the self, not to others. The restless free thinker must never be content with themselves, with the person they are today. "Never keep back or bury in silence what can be thought against your thoughts!", he wrote in *Daybreak*. "It is among the foremost requirements of honesty of thought. Every day you must conduct your campaign also against yourself" (D 370).

This approach puts him in the tradition of the Stoics and the ancient Spartans, and although he wasn't an ascetic — quite the reverse, in the *The Genealogy of Morals* he criticised the ideology of severe self-discipline for its own sake for actually negating life and encouraging self-hatred — his life and outlook today would today be called Puritan. After his university days, Nietzsche didn't drink alcohol, loathing the Germans on account of their beer guzzling. "No eating between meals, no coffee: coffee makes gloomy. *Tea* beneficial only in the morning", was his dietary advice (EH WIASC) (although he wasn't averse to intoxication. Owing to increasing blindness and headaches, Nietzsche dosed himself with chloral hydrate, a hypnotic opiate, and there is some speculation that this contributed to his breakdown.)

Forever a man of paradoxes, Nietzsche was both deeply radical and profoundly conservative. He advised us to go beyond yet much of his advice is age-old. The notion that suffering can be good for you by strengthening the character would be recognised by the Stoics. It is the backbone of the traditional English public school system and used to be the kind of thing children were routinely taught at Christian Sunday School. The idea that toil and persistence are fundamental to creation will be recognised by any authors and any people whose profession involves creation and invention (think of James Dyson, who in 1983 invented the world's first bagless vacuum cleaner, after five years and 5,127 prototypes). "What is written without effort is in general read without pleasure", as Dr. Johnson said, a sentiment echoed by Nietzsche: "it's hard to write well... no one has a good style by nature... you really have to work like a dog to get one" (Fuss & Shapiro, 1971, p. 6).

In his determination to become the best, Nietzsche became one of the most beguiling writers in German literature, who demands that we become the best. As Karl Jaspers observed of his writing and philosophy: "no matter whether desolation keeps overcoming the reader's initially fascinated soul, he will still be affected by something in this constant conquest, this striving for more, this reaching for the stars. We are driven out of every position we may have taken— that is, out of everything finite. We are flung *into a whirlpool*" (Jaspers, 1961, p. 87).

Sometimes it's difficult to remember that suffering is the norm in life. In the age of social media one-upmanship, in which everyone else on Facebook is smiling, always on holiday and generally having a wonderful life, it's perhaps harder than ever to keep in mind that happiness isn't the norm. Everyone has problems, and in truth, most people actually have it worse than you. Judging your everyday life by the semi-fictional standards of social media is like comparing your love-life to a rom-com.

Those who expect happiness are guaranteed never to attain it. As Douglas Adams said: "A life that is burdened with expectations is a heavy life. Its fruit is sorrow and disappointment." Happiness is not and nor should it be a goal, but a consequence. It is what results after you have toiled, overcome obstacles, achieved your aims through blood, sweat and tears. And then doing it all over again. As Chumbawumba sang in *Tubthumping*: "I get knocked down / But I get up again / You're never gonna keep me down." Happiness comes through embracing, employing and then overcoming stress, anxiety and depression.

3

Live Dangerously!
Safe spaces

Ours is an age which puts "safety first", whether it be through risk assessments at work, the much dreaded and sometimes mythologised "health 'n' safety" brigade, the precautionary principle in the field of science or "safe spaces" on university campuses. Ours is a time in which to give "offence" is a grievous transgression, and in which people are easily "traumatised" by contrary or hurtful ideas in university lectures, or day-to-day encounters in the form of "microaggressions". Hence trigger warnings on books to protect the vulnerable, and teachers no longer blowing whistles in school playgrounds lest they upset children. Hence, too, students being permitted to absent themselves from lectures in which they might be "distressed" by contro-versial topics. The young seem especially delicate in these safety-seeking times, with a report from July 2016 finding almost half of voters aged 18 to 24 cried or felt like crying when they heard that the UK had voted to leave the Euro-pean Union (*Guardian*, 02/07/16). This is what they call "Generation Snowflake" (because they "melt" so easily).

Nietzsche would regard the quest for safety as a negation of life, demands for "health and safety" as a ludicrous barrier to the free spirit of inquiry and exploration. Life necessitated strife and struggle. We must live dangerously. Children seek risk to test their limits and to extend their limits—witness how infants will walk on walls and climb trees. Life demands that we take risks and place ourselves in sometimes mortal peril. The ascent of Everest, the discovery of the New World, men on the Moon: such achievements were made by those who embraced risk. "The devotion of the greatest is to encounter risk and danger and play dice for death", spoke Zarathustra (TSZ OSO). Galileo offended the Papacy with his quest for truth, Darwin offended many with the theory of evolution. Sometimes there is an imperative to be offensive. As a young Nietzsche wrote to his sister: "if you wish to strive for peace of soul and pleasure, then believe; if you wish to be a devotee of truth, then inquire" (letter to his sister, 11/06/65; quoted in Kaufmann, 1974, p. 21). Nietzsche would laugh in the face of "safe spaces". He would urge that we create "dangerous spaces". As he summed it up in 1888: "It is no small advantage to live under a hundred swords of Damocles: that way one learns to dance, one attains 'freedom of movement'" (WTP 771).

Nietzsche called "the essence of life… the priority of the spontaneous, attacking, overcoming, reinterpreting, restructuring and shaping forces" (OTGM 2.12). The truly free, joyful man is one who lives without foundations or walls in a permanent and perpetual state of doubt. "Who will prove the strongest? The most moderate, those who need no extreme tenets of faith" (cited in Jaspers, 1961, p. 94). This dangerous undertaking required fortitude. "The desire for a strong faith is *not* the proof of a strong faith, rather the opposite. *If one has it* one may permit oneself the beautiful luxury of scepticism: one is secure enough, firm enough, fixed enough" (TOTI EUM 12). As Camus later wrote: "Nietzsche does not flinch. He answers and his answer is bold: Damocles never danced better than beneath the sword. One must accept the unacceptable and contend the untenable" (Camus, 2000, p. 45).

Yet it was paradoxical that in real life Nietzsche, his wretched health aside, in material terms lived a rather comfortable existence by most people's standards, by beaches in Italy or in the Swiss Alps. "What did Nietzsche ever risk, really risk? A few bad reviews? Getting lost on one of his Alpine walks? An occasional drug overdose?", asks Richard C. Soloman in *Living With Nietzsche* (2003). "The death-defying images do not hide the fact that Nietzsche was sickly all of his life. His celebration of 'health' as a philosopher, seems pathetic, at best" (Soloman, 2003, p. 32). Although we can sympathise with the power fantasies of a weak and handicapped failed writer, his strong counsel to live dangerously as a Superman jars with what we know about Nietzsche as a man. A needy, mild-mannered provincial German, strolling along mountain paths holding an umbrella to protect his feeble eyes from the sun: Conan the Barbarian he was not.

Still, this still doesn't detract from the essence of his cry to "Live Dangerously". As with much that Nietzsche wrote, of wars and struggle, he was speaking metaphorically. He was giving intellectual advice. When he urges us to go to war or embrace danger he is talking about our approach to ideas, our outlook, our convictions and our beliefs. To live danger-ously means not to shy from thoughts and words. It is his call to freedom, to liberate oneself from ideology, to be strong—and then, only after all that, to be happy. "One must never have spared oneself, harshness must be among one's habits, if one is to be happy and cheerful among nothing but hard truths" (EH WIWSGB.3).

He would find our culture of health and safety life-denying, certainly in academia where the demand for safe spaces goes hand-in-hand with censorious cries of "no platform" for people who utter the objectionable. The desire for safety and the impulse for censorship are intimately linked; Ray Bradbury's dystopian novel *Fahrenheit 451* reminds us of the symbiotic relationship between the two. In the story, books are burnt not because they are deemed to contain subversive ideas, but because they make people unhappy. They hurt people's feelings. The book-burning police chief Beatty explains himself thus: "Coloured people don't like *Little Black Sambo*. Burn it. White people don't feel good about *Uncle Tom's Cabin*. Burn It." He continues: "You must understand that our civilisation is so vast that we can't have our minorities upset and stirred. Ask yourself, What do we want in this country, above all? People want to be happy, isn't that right?... That's all we live for, isn't it? For pleasure and titillation? And you must admit our culture provides plenty of these" (Bradbury, 1970, pp. 62–63). The desire for the happiness of all demands the silence of people who rock the boat. Comfort means compromising liberty. To live safely means to live in a prison. This is why Nietzsche always put freedom before safety.

Nietzsche wouldn't be surprised that the biggest detractors of freedom today are often the young, especially "no platform" students, or those who call for the results of referendums to be overturned. He'd be unsurprised because Nietzsche saw universities as inherently hostile to free thought. After leaving the academy, like Schopenhaeur, Nietzsche developed a very low opinion of university education and of tenured professors. Knowledge under control of the state, in the form of universities, so Nietzsche believed, would ultimately be shaped to serve the state. "The man who consents to be a state philosopher, must also consent to be regarded as renouncing the search for truth in all its secret retreats. At any rate, so long as he enjoys his position, he must recognise something higher than truth—the state" (UM 4 viii).

In his times, certainly, Nietzsche believed that education had become a servant of Prussian state. "What is the task of all higher education?—To turn a man into a machine" (TOTI). Education was valued for how useful it would be, not for opening up minds. This is partly, too, why Nietzsche constantly inveighed against his fellow philosopher Immanuel Kant, who he called "the great Chinaman of Königsberg" (BGE 210), a teasing slur, as Nietzsche associated Oriental philosophy with moral rigidity, mediocrity and conceitedness (see "How 'Chinese' was Kant?", Steve Palmquist, *The Philosopher*, vol. LXXXIV no. 1,

Spring 1996). "Kant held to his university, submitted to its regulations, and belonged, as his colleagues and students thought, to a definite religious faith: and naturally his example has produced, above all, University professors of philosophy", Nietzsche wrote in his 1874. For Nietzsche, academic professors were conformist, conservative herd-men who are hostile to novelty, experiment and adventure.

Hence, he would not be surprised at the current state of American and British universities and their "safe spaces". As the University of Kent's Joanna Williams outlines in her book *Academic Freedom in an Age of Conformity* (2016): "many students have come to expect freedom from speech. They argue the university campus should be a 'safe space', free from emotional harm or potential offence." Their tutors are often little better. "Today, far from championing academic freedom, we see examples of scholars seeking to keep debates away from the public or to censor views which they personally find politically objectionable" (Williams, 2016, pp. 4, 10). Universities have long since surrendered their roles as places of free thinking. This explains the rise of think-tanks in the past thirty years, to provide avenues through which new ideas can be discussed and exchanged freely. Nietzsche's advice to students might be not merely to abolish "safe spaces" but avoid academia altogether. "A really radical living for truth just isn't possible in a university", he wrote (Fuss & Shapiro, 1971, p. 14).

Universities, however, are only a microcosm of a wider malaise, one laid out in Claire Fox's 2016 book, *I Find That Offensive*. In it, Fox explains how the ostensible appeal for civility and good manners have become marshalled as tools of censorship. She points out, for instance, that while Islamists and feminists may seem to have little in common, they are both united in demanding retribution in the form of bans, penalties and censorship of those who hurt their feelings. Safety-seeking and the enforced silencing of others are two sides of the same coin.

This is not to berate the young. It is the fault of their elders—my generation. Our safety-obsessed, so-called "Snowflake" generation grew up in the 1990s and first decade of this century, in an environment of "health and safety". They were taught at school that slights they received were tantamount to bullying or emotional abuse that would forever traumatise them. It's no wonder they are scared of new or challenging ideas, demanding censorship of those who might cause them distress, regarding every counter-argument as "hate speech". Nietzsche taught us contrari-wise. Only sticks and stones will break your bones. New words and challenging ideas won't kill you. They might even make you stronger.

4

Convictions are prisons
Religious fundamentalism

One of the main thrusts of the Enlightenment, if not its central tenet, was the belief that religion and the supernatural would gradually ebb away and then disappear as mankind employed reason in his quest for knowledge and improvement. The attack on the World Trade Center in September 2001 was confirmation that this Enlightenment hope was misplaced and that the certitudes of religious belief remain as tenacious as ever. God is clearly not dead. But Nietzsche didn't oppose Christianity from the point of view of a rationalist, a humanist or an atheist. He was none of these things because he wasn't any "-ist". Nietzsche wasn't so much against religious belief itself, but belief in general—in any "-ism". He opposed all convictions, all ideologies and all dogmas. "Convictions are more dangerous enemies of truth than lies" (HATH 483). It is people who have firmly-held beliefs who are the worst, as Yeats's poem elaborates. It is people who have righteousness on their side who are the ones to watch.

Convictions are the consequence of sticking to beliefs, and one of the motives for beliefs is the desire for power. *"The demon of power.*—Not necessity, not desire—no, the love of power is the demon of men. Let them have everything—health, food, a place to live, entertainment—they are and remain unhappy and low-spirited: for the demon waits and waits and will be satisfied" (D 262). Nietzsche would today recognise the combination of self-righteousness and resentment of the Islamist suicide bomber who hates a rich, successful Western culture—a culture superior to an Arab world that has been in decline since the Middle Ages. The jihadist also hates the Jews for being rich. Deprived of success or women, he dreams of 72 virgins in paradise: "he who wants to acquire the feeling of power resorts to any means and disdains nothing that will nourish it. He who has it, however, has become very fastidious and noble in his tastes; he now finds few things to satisfy him" (D 165). The nihilist jihadist hates life in the here and the now, but is possessed of certitude and righteousness in his journey towards the next.

The Christian, too, promises a blissful afterlife, in the beyond, because he can't guarantee happiness in this life. Hence, argued Nietzsche, Christianity rejects life. "Oh, how much superfluous cruelty and vivisection have proceeded from those religions which invented sin! And from those people who desired by means of it to gain the highest enjoyment of their power!" (D 34). Christianity is the religion for the mob, for the weak and resentful who are unable to achieve greatness. "The preponderance of feelings of displeasure over feelings of pleasure is the *cause* of a fictitious morality and religion" (TAC 15). Its success lies in appealing to common denominators.

Nietzsche thought that Christianity was based on resentment of the powerful: "the evangel preached to the power and lowly, the collective rebellion of everything downtrodden, wretched, ill-constituted, under privileged" (TOTI TIM 4). It negates life, asking us to be humble and the same, to be happy with our lot. "Christianity appealed as a preservative force, it simply strengthened that natural and very strong instinct of all the weak which bids them protect, maintain, and mutually support each other. What is Christian 'virtue' and 'love of men,' if not precisely this mutual assistance with a view survival, this solidarity of the weak… What is Christian altruism, if it is not the mob-egotism of the weak which divines that, if everybody looks after everybody else, every individual will be preserved for a longer period of time" (WTP 246).

Christianity for him was a mutual aid society, its morality merely a survival technique. "What is 'virtue' and 'charity' in Christianity if not just this mutual preservation, this solidarity of the weak" (WTP 246). You should love your neighbour in order that he love you back. Or, I'll promise to scratch your back if you scratch mine. Hence Christian ethics scarcely embody authentic morality. Christian teaching is a paradoxically amoral, self-centred doctrine: "love of one's neighbour, living for others and other things *can* be the defensive measure for the preservation of the sternest selfishness" (EH WIASC.9).

Today, he would call Christian morality a successful evolutionary adaptive system: "judgments of 'good' and 'evil' sum up experiences of what is 'expedient' and 'inexpedient'. One holds that what is called good preserves the species, while what is called evil harms the species" (TJS 4). He saw morality and truth as having no transcendental worth, but adapted to help in the survival of the tribe. In *The Joyous Science*, in the section "Origin of knowledge", Nietzsche writes: "Gradually, the human brain became full of such judgments and convictions, and a ferment, a struggle, and lust for power developed in this tangle. Not only utility and delight but every kind of impulse took sides in this fight about 'truths'" (TJS 110).

Nietzsche's writings emerged in an intellectual climate that was dominated by Darwinian ideas of survival and evolution, but Nietzsche was not a Darwinist, despite super-ficial resemblances, with his recurring themes of "struggle" and "improvement". Darwinians came to measure evolu-tionary success in terms of quantity, while Nietzsche believed in the improvement of the quality of man. Darwin talked about the survival and evolution of species, whereas

Nietzsche was concerned about individuals. And in the end, the needs of the many conflict with the desire and greatness of the individual. This is why Nietzsche decried Christianity, and this is why he would have been horrified by the Third Reich, with its herd-like conformity, mass rallies, pack mentality and rhetoric of the "master race". Nietzsche rejected Darwin's idea of species merely surviving as biological entities; he wanted men to live as higher spirits. If anything, Nietzsche's thought owes more to the spirit of Jean-Baptiste Lamarck, in that he believed individuals could advance and evolve through their own efforts.

Religions allow men merely to survive and propagate by number, rather than to truly live. One of Christianity's, and indeed Islam's, evolutionary tactics has to create sin, that is, to punish individuals who deviate from the accepted mores of the tribe. Morality and punitive monotheism were chanced upon by accident in order to help these tribes survive, reproduce and proselytise. Sin and punishment were created to deter deviants who threatened the well-being and prospects of the tribe. "The community is fundamentally an alliance between the weak against the strong aggressor, and disgrace is an important defensive weapon. Punishment is not merely retaliation. Treated as an inferior or outsider by the group, the offender is implicitly and threateningly reminded of natural ferocity, of conditions prevailing at less advanced stages of civilization" (Wand. s.22). Christianity involved instilling conformity in order to temper our impulses. Christianity intoxicated and seduced us into becoming satisfied, by removing pain, by giving answers: "To trace something unknown back to something known is alleviating, soothing, gratifying and gives moreover a feeling of power. Danger, disquiet, anxiety attend the unknown — the first instinct is to *eliminate* these distressing states. First principle: any explanation is better than none" (TOTI TFGE 5).

This was Nietzsche's essential accusation against Christianity, that it makes for a safe and stable society, is the main reason why people have always felt frightened by his attacks on morality. A traditional method of attacking Nietzsche is to quote, or more commonly paraphrase, Fyodor Dostoyevsky's *Brothers Karamazov* (1879–80), where one brother asks: "Without God and the future life? It means everything is permitted now, one can do anything?" In other words, goes the insinuation, a Godless world would lead to moral anarchy, chaos and destruction. Godlessness gives a green light to libertinage. But one might as well turn the question around and ask: "If there *is* a God, is everything permitted?" It's the very belief in God that has justified anything. Wars, genocide, ethnic cleansing, persecution: all have been carried out throughout history with God's sanction, by the righteous, by those infused with a strong sense of right and wrong, of good and evil. Warmongers, jihadists and those who kill in the name of a belief always do so in the belief that good is on their side.

"I regard Christianity as the most fatal seductive lie that has yet existed, as the greatest unholy lie", he wrote (WTP 200). Yet the self-described "antichrist" had a focus far beyond than that. Nietzsche believed that secular believers could be even worse than Christians. Nietzsche predicted that in a new age after the death of God, after Christianity had finally perished, morality would become even more brutal. "Those who have abandoned God cling that much more firmly to the faith in morality", he wrote (WTP 18). Morals that have divine sanction are strong, with explicit threat of damnation for deviants and rewards to adherents. Morality devoid of God therefore demands greater punishment. When there is no threat of eternal damnation in the afterlife, why fear being immoral? When it becomes more tempting to break society's rules, the deterrence must be greater. This is why, before the invention of police forces, criminals would be hanged for petty crimes.

This is why Nietzsche foresaw a terrifying, nihilistic future: "the time when anger will constitute the real male emotion… politics will become more fantastic and partisan than ever" (HATH 425). He wouldn't have been surprised by the horrors of atheistic totalitarianism. It is the least religious men who become the most fanatic. "The place one is most certain to find idealist theories is with unreflexive practical men; for their reputation requires and idealist luster" (HATH 328). With right on your side, anything is committed. The same crimes have been committed by communists, fascists and democrats. Why, when Britain's former Prime Minister was asked, did Tony Blair decide to invade Iraq? "Because it was the right thing to do."

Religious believer or non-religious believer, Nietzsche made no fundamental difference: it is those who live with certitudes and beliefs who are the worst types. "The great conquerors have always mouthed the pathetic language of virtue: they have had around them asses in a condition of elevation who wanted to hear only the most elevated language. Strange madness of moral judgements" (D 189). Nietzsche was alert to the eternal pull of ideology and conviction, the manifestation of the malign Will to Power. This appeal transcends religion. Convictions emerge from the natural desire for power. "Out of passions grow opinions; mental sloth lets these rigidify into convictions" (HATH 637).

Ideology may cause people to kill in the name of "right", sure, but ideology can be so strong that it can cause people to lay down their life for it, too. The heretic may die for his beliefs, his executioner kills for his. Both are stupid and both are wrong. And it's this willingness to kill and to die for convictions that has seduced people into believing the ultimate action is a seal of its veracity: "Martyrdoms", he writes in *The Anti-Christ*, "have been a great misfortune in history: they have *seduced*... The inference of all idiots... that a cause for which someone is willing to die... must have something in it—this inference has become an unspeakable drag on verification... Martyrs have *harmed* truth" (TAC 53).

Nietzsche was never entirely happy settling for the term atheist for this very reason, as atheism is an appeal to certitude and finality. We find the idea of an atheist bible or atheist temple a bit silly and incongruous, but to Nietzsche they would be logical. As he wrote in *Twilight of the Idols*. "I mistrust all systemizers and avoid them. The will to a system is a lack of integrity" (TOTI MA 26). He called atheists "these 'unbelievers'... opposition to this ideal seems to be their very last article of faith, they are so earnest on this point, so passionate their words, their gestures then become — but does this necessarily make what they believe *true*?... We 'seekers after knowledge' are suspicious of virtually every kind of believer... a strong belief which 'makes one blessed' arouses suspicion of what is believed" (GOM 3.24). Nietzsche is never satisfied. Nietzsche was the eternal critic. He writes of the requirement "to question further, more deeply, severely, harshly, evilly and quietly than one had questioned heretofore" (TJS 3). He wasn't so much interested in answers as with questions.

To adhere to a religion is to adhere to someone else's belief system, to be means to another man's ends. "Convictions are prisons" (TAC 54), he said. "The snake that cannot slough its skin, perishes. Likewise spirits which are prevented from changing their opinions; they cease to be spirits" (D 573). Man must constantly fight the force that pulls him towards convictions. Nietzsche called for constant inward struggle and self-overcoming: "if one feels he is a free, restlessly lively mind, he can prevent this rigidity through constant change" (HATH 637). One must avoid stasis or complacency. Nietzsche acclaims eternal self-doubt and war against certainty and oneself. "A very popular error: having the courage of one's convictions; rather it is a matter of having the courage for an attack on one's convictions!!!" (Spring 1888, cited in Kaufmann, 1974, p.19).

5

The sick,
loud gesture
Virtue signalling

The term "virtue signalling", an action by which you declare how much you love or hate something principally in order to improve your social standing, was coined in April 2015 (*The Spectator* 18/04/15). Yet it describes something ancient to humanity: doing or saying something that sounds altruistic in order to improve one's social standing. Only through the shrinking of the globe through technology, especially in our digital age, has less-than-genuine ostentatious compassion become more evident and prolific — what with social media providing the platform for the multitude to profess their virtuous credentials.

In Britain, this usually involves declaring one's support for the National Health Service, the BBC and gay marriage, or by wearing an Aids ribbon or a remembrance day poppy all year round — or even, after the country's referendum to leave the EU in June 2016, a safety pin to declare one's non-racist goodness. As opposed to conspicuous compassion, one can display one's virtue through publically hating figures that polite society deems it acceptable to dislike. One can pronounce one's detestation of the Tories, Rupert Murdoch, Nigel Farage or Donald Trump.

Although the digital age has indeed made virtue signalling far easier, it is not an inherently new phenomenon.

Before social media, at the turn of the millennium and the late-20th century there was "conspicuous compassion" in which people sported empathy ribbons, cried in public or went to Live Aid in very public displays of kindness and caring (West, 2004). And long before any of this we had the Pharisees, condemned in the Bible for their superficial self-righteousness.

Virtue signalling is another form of group-think, of the herd in action. Nietzsche decried loud declarations of virtue, "that Pharisee tactic of the sick, the *loud* gesture, whose favourite part is that of 'righteous indignation'... this hoarse indignant bark of the sickly dog, the biting, rabid deceit of such 'righteous' Pharisees" (GOM 3.14). Nietzsche denounced compassion and humanitarianism, especially public displays of such emotions, because he didn't believe in humanity or "people". He didn't see people in terms of collectives: he only saw individuals. "Not 'mankind' but *overman* is the goal!" (WTP 1001). He recognised that people who profess to love "humanity" tend not to actually like human beings. As Camus wrote: "humanitarian feelings are always accompanied by misanthropy. Humanity is loved in general in order to avoid loving anybody in particular" (Camus, 2000, p. 6).

It's logical that Nietzsche, who has a reputation for exalting cruelty and decrying compassion, should excoriate Rousseau, who "loved" humanity (Camus, 2000, p. 6). Nietzsche, that arch individualist and anti-ideologist, never sees people as part of general abstractions. Although he had much in common with Karl Marx—nationality, money problems, a duelling scar, imposing facial hair, disciples who misunderstood the master very badly indeed—he fundamentally disagreed with Marx's emphasis on class struggle. For Nietzsche it was all about the individual. That's also why Nietzsche so violently disagreed with Rousseau, who, like Marx, was also co-opted by those who erected totalitarian regimes and who believed in "humanity".

Nietzsche was against public emoting because it represented a surrender to our baser, darker irrational urges, the dark side of the Will to Power. Although he was treasured by late 19th-century decadents who confused him for a Romantic, what with his highly literary philosophy and his volcanic and pungent rhetoric, Nietzsche was not an irrationalist. In *Human, All Too Human,* Nietzsche exhorts the values of: "Rigorous reflection, compression, coldness, plainness… restraint of feeling and taciturnity" (HATH 195).

Nietzsche believed in truth, albeit of a highly unstable, contingent, perspectival and disposable variety. He believed in constant experimentation and argument. This is why we had to struggle. Truths were to be obtained but they were always to be contingently held, ready to be jettisoned. Far from being a casual relativist, Nietzsche believed we had to cross swords in the struggle for truth because it mattered so dearly. "Truth has had to be fought for every step of the way, almost everything else dear to our hearts, on which our love and our trust in life depend, had to be sacrificed to it" (TAC 50). As Walter Kaufmann explains: "Nietzsche's valuation of suffering and cruelty was not the consequence of any gory irrationalism, but a corollary of his high esteem of rationality. The powerful man is the rational man who subjects even his most cherished faith to the severe scrutiny of reason and is prepared to give up his beliefs if they cannot stand this stern test. He abandons what he loves most, if rationality requires it. He does not yield to his inclinations and impulses" (Kaufmann, 1974, p. 244).

This stance was at its most evident during Nietzsche's "middle period" from 1878 to 1882, comprising the books *Human, All Too Human, Daybreak* and *The Joyous Science.* Nietzsche's writing during these years was at its most inquisitive and doubtful, or "affirmative" and "benevolent", as he put it (EH TGS), before his work took its final bombastic, messianic turn. As he wrote in his most under-rated and least excitingly entitled book, *Daybreak*: "Every smallest step in the field of free thinking, and of the personally formed life, has ever been fought for at a cost of spiritual and physical tortures… change has required its innumerable martyrs… Nothing has been bought more dearly than that little bit of human reason and sense of freedom that is now the basis of our pride" (D 18).

Of the first book of the doubting, pensive "middle period", *Human, All Too Human*, Nietzsche later claimed that "there is significance in the fact that it is actually the hundredth anniversary of the death of Voltaire which the book as it were apologizes for being published in 1878. For Voltaire is, in contrast to all who have written after him, above all a grandseigneur of the spirit: precisely what I am too" (EH HATH 1). That Nietzsche should see himself a descendent of Voltaire, that epitome of Enlightenment reason and humanity, should not surprise us. Voltaire was the free-thinker par excellence of the Enlightenment, he who dared to challenge received wisdom. In the same spirit of the Enlightenment, Nietzsche attacked superstition, religious dogma and uncritical and outdated ways of thinking. Nietzsche represented a continuation of Voltaire's spirit of criticism and progress. "Voltaire still comprehended *umanità* in the Renaissance," noted Nietzsche, "the cause of taste, of science, of the arts, of progress itself and civilization" (WTP 100).

But Nietzsche's professed admiration for Voltaire in 1878 was a calculating gesture, too, designed to antagonise Wagner, who was still smarting from the terrible reception to his works in France. Nietzsche knew that that such a dedication would hasten and complete the break with his former master, who had now, to Nietzsche's grave disappointment, appeared to have reconciled himself with Christianity in *Parsifal*. As Eric Heller wrote in *The Importance of Nietzsche* (1988): "Voltaire served Nietzsche merely as the stick with which to chastise Wagner. The composer had only to look at the work's dedication to Voltaire to suspect that it was meant as an insult to him or, if not as an insult, as a defiant declaration of independence" (Heller, 1988, p. 60).

Even if his Voltairean period was transient, Nietzsche certainly wasn't a Romantic. In *Human, All Too Human*, Nietzsche denounces Jean-Jacques Rousseau, a founder figure of naive Romanticism that, as Edmund Burke had predicted, would lead to tyranny. In it, Nietzsche writes: "It is not Voltaire's temperate nature, inclined to organizing, cleansing and restructuring, but rather Rousseau's passionate idiocies and half-truths that have called awake the optimistic spirit of revolution, counter to which I shout: '*Ecrasez l'infame!*' ['crush the infamous thing' — Voltaire's letter to d'Alembert Nov 28, 1762, referring to superstition]. Because of him, the spirit of the enlightenment and of progressive development has been scared off for a long time to come: let us see (each one for himself) whether it is not possible to call it back again!" (HATH 463).

Far from acclaiming or venerating the emotions of compassion, intuition and introspection, as Romantics do, Nietzsche believed that unmastered, indulged emotions were at the root of dangerous convictions. "In all ages, one has taken 'beautiful feelings' for arguments, the 'heaving bosom' for the bellows the divinity, convictions for a 'criterion of truth,' the need of an opponent for a question mark against wisdom: this falsehood, this counterfeiting, permeates the whole history of philosophy" (WTP 414).

Today, he would observe the sly, ultimately self-centred goal of the virtue signaller or those who abound loudly with piety. "He that humbleth himself shall be exalted", said St Luke. Nietzsche reversed this to become "He who humbleth himself wants to be exalted" (HATH 1 87). Nietzsche wouldn't be a fan of BBC *Question Time*, for instance, with its audience members' tendency towards self-righteous indignation as they inveigh against the Tories because they want to "save the NHS". He would deplore the cry of the metropolitan liberal who wants to draw attention to his compassionate credentials through enjoyable self-flagellation.

Nietzsche would have immediately recognised the false modesty of Harry Enfield and Paul Whitehouse's radio DJ personas, Smashey and Nicey, who do a lot of work for *charidee*, "but don't like to talk about it". He would have ridiculed, too, the guest who appeared on the fictional news programme, *The Day Today*, to boast she has raised fifteen hundred pounds for a jam festival. "Fifteen hundred pounds? That's a pathetic amount of money!", replies her interrogator, Chris Morris. "The only reason you've done it is to make yourself look important. How dare you come on this programme saying 'Oh look at me I'm raising fifteen hundred pounds for the homeless'."

Nietzsche abhorred boastful displays of compassion and the desire to be valued by others. Nietzsche would regard virtue signalling as feeble and needy, that desire for affirmation by others. Why be slave to the opinions of others? "Better to be a fool on one's own account than a wise man at the approval of others!" (TSZ TL). So what if you care about the NHS? And so what of your feelings? Maybe the only person you care about is you. It is the compassionate and those with convictions — the believers in their righteousness, religious and secular — who are the most selfish. They are the worst types, said Nietzsche: "whatever harm the world-calumniators may do, *the harm the good do is the most harmful harm*" (EH WIAD.4).

6

The herd instinct
Twitterstorms

Like ostentatious caring that doesn't so much change the world as make attention-seekers feel better about themselves, mob rule is also as old as the hills. But what we have seen since the advent of social media in the past ten years is conspicuous compassion and the fury of the mob coalesce and reinforce each other. The most palpable manifestation is that of the "Twitterstorm". This ensues when a public figure says something controversial or unfashionable and is met with howls of outrage by social media users, who demand he or she apologise for their "offensive" comments. This usually results in a grudging and half-hearted show of atonement by the author, actor or journalist that generated it. Or else, people find themselves demeaned and attacked on social media for having unfashionable and incorrect views.

This heady combination of self-righteousness and bullying would have disgusted Nietzsche. He would have recognised in herd-like Twitterstorms for their "Lustful greed, bitter envy, sour vindictiveness, mob pride" (TSZ TVB). He would also recognise the sadistic pleasure derived by mass, online moralising: "every poor devil finds pleasure in scolding—it gives him a little of the intoxication of power. Even complaining and wailing can give life a charm for the sake of which one endures it: there is a small dose of *revenge* in every complaint, one reproaches those who are different for one's feeling vile..." (TOTI EOAUM 34).

Nietzsche hated democracy because he believed it relied upon conformity. His life-affirming scepticism was designed for those able and willing to transcend the doctrines of the masses, the "herd instinct". The herd possesses morality, the rules of the herd, to help the tribe survive. "Morality is herd instinct in the individual" (TJS 116). Thus anyone who wants to survive in the tribe and prosper within it must obey its mores and customs.

This is why Nietzsche didn't believe in objective morality. There exists no external perspective upon life, nothing above life, no privileged viewpoint. This life here is all there is and we make of it what we will and can. There is no God, no eternal, transcendental good or bad, only merely survival techniques that present themselves — masquerade — as right or wrong. "Morality as an illusion of the species, designed to motivate the individuals to sacrifice himself to the future: apparently allowing him an infinite value, so that by means of this self-consciousness he should tyrannize over and keep down other sides of his nature" (WTP 404). Those who blaspheme or contravene society's mores must therefore be punished by the tribe. In retribution, the tribe and the herd derives a pleasurable feeling: "In the act of cruelty the community refreshes itself and for once throws off the gloom of constant fear and caution. Cruelty is one of the oldest joys of mankind" (D 18).

Societies — that is, tribes writ large — will necessarily have rules, codes and taboos. Tribes always punish those who transgress norms, who blaspheme, who threaten. Were social media around in 1950s America, no doubt it would be used to name and shame communists. In Britain in times past there might have been Twitterstorms about Catholics. And maybe that would have been a good thing. Catholics and communists were indeed a threat to the USA and UK at one time. While the urge to castigate is universal, our targets shift according to changing taboos. Nietzsche recognised that once a society becomes liberal in one area of morality it erects taboos to replace them. As he observed in *Thus Spoke*

Zarathustra, anticipating the environmentalist movement at its most extreme fringe: "Once blasphemy against God was the greatest blasphemy, but God died, and thereupon these blasphemers died too. To blaspheme the earth is now the most dreadful offence, and to esteem the bowels of the Inscrutable more highly than the meaning of the earth" (TSZ PROL).

Taboos change over space and time. One time it was normal to be homophobic and abhor religious swear words, where now a kind of mutual reversal has taken place. In the Western world in the 21st century, the greatest taboos are racism, homophobia and sexism. Making a transgression in any of these areas today could cost you your job and certainly earn you public shaming.

It's not only the obvious intolerance we see online towards today's secular blasphemers. We internalise the power of our moral guardians. It's that internalised power which means you think twice before speaking up in public on issues about race or religion. It's why you didn't admit to friends or colleagues that you voted Brexit. It's the same power that has left so many Tweets untweeted for fear of losing face or one's job.

Of course, there is nothing admirable about racism, homophobia or sexism. But there's nothing laudable about mob rule, either, about the liberal-Left telling you to shut up because you have unfashionable views. There is nothing noble about deriving satisfaction from telling others what they can and can't say. Mob rule is a fierce, intolerable spectacle and goes beyond Left and Right. As Nietzsche put it in *Beyond Good and Evil*: "Madness is something rare in individuals — but in groups, parties, peoples, ages it is the rule" (BGE 156).

That above quote is often quoted on social media. And there is something ironic about counter-Twitterstorms, instigated by libertarians or those on the alt-Right, where a different mob will make a counter-attack by quoting Nietzsche himself. "The liberal Left mob are just virtue signalling", comes the collective cry, without irony. "Nietzsche hated mobs", says the herd. This communal veneration for an arch-individualist is ironic, and there has always been the tendency to regard Nietzsche as a prophet himself. It's a paradox that brings to mind the scene in *Monty Python's Life of Brian* where the protagonist pleads with the crowd:

Brian: You don't need to follow anybody! You've got to think for yourselves! You're all individuals!

Crowd: Yes! We're all individuals!

Brian: You're all different!

Crowd: Yes! We are all different!

Man in crowd: I'm not…

Nietzsche would have be that sole voice of dissent in the crowd.

Although Nietzsche craved attention and recognition as a thinker and a writer, he ultimately would have abhorred being thought of as a prophet, for his words to be treated as gospel. Even, privately, when he confessed that he did seek followers of a kind, he typically and appropriately wished a kind of anti-disciple, writing in 1887: "*Type of my disciples —* To those human beings who are of any concern to me I wish suffering, desolation, sickness, ill-treatment, indignities — I wish that they should not remain unfamiliar with profound self-contempt, the torture of self-mistrust, the wretchedness of the vanquished: I have no pity for them, because I wish them the only thing that can prove today whether one is worth anything or not — that one endures" (WTP 910). Karl Jaspers believed that Nietzsche "does not show us the way, he does not teach us a faith, he gives us nothing to stand on. Instead, he grants us no peace, torments us ceaselessly, hunts us out of every retreat, and forbids all concealment… by plunging us into nothingness that he wants to create for us the vastness of space" (Jaspers, 1961, p. 104).

What would he think about his name being invoked today to lend authority to an argument? It's hard to say, but he would shirk from those "wise words" memes that do the rounds on social media, intended to convey a sense of great wisdom, especially those bearing his face and his words: "*Being profound and seeming profound.* — Those who know that they are profound strive for clarity. Those who would like to seem profound to the crowd strive for obscurity" (GS 173). He would have preferred to have been recognised as an anti-prophet, as a master we would follow in order ultimately to reject. To be truly Nietzschean one must paradoxically attack what he says. His only imperative is fulfil your inner potential and be one's only judge and master.

Only the weak need to rely on the rules of others, or the crowd. "It is not the ferocity of the beast of prey that requires a moral disguise but the herd animal with its profound mediocrity, timidity" (TJS 352). Nietzsche believed the creative man of genius would construct his own rules. This didn't mean becoming a nihilist, in believing in nothing, but by creating one's own rules in erecting one's own something. As Kaufmann elaborates: "The great artist does not stick to any established code; yet his work is not lawless but has structure and form. Beethoven did not conform to the rules of Haydn or Mozart; yet his symphonies have form throughout" (Kaufmann, 1974, p. 250).

Nietzsche warned against nihilism as an end, but he saw it as necessary transition. "This man of the future, who will redeem us as much from the previous ideal as from *what was bound to grow out of it*, from the great disgust, from the will to nothingness, from nihilism, this midday stroke of the bell, this toll of great decision, which once again liberates the will, which once again gives the earth its goal and man his hope, this Antichristian and Antinihilist, this conqueror of God and of nothingness — *he must come one day*" (GOM 2.24). Unfortunately he was unclear about what was to replace the crumbling morality based on a Christianity that was losing its authority. This lack of prescription was perhaps intended:

we would have to find our own way without yet another prophet to tell us how.

Yet there are some standards of humanity he clearly does value. He is not quite the immoralist he sometimes professed to be, or who we have been led to understand. In *Beyond Good and Evil* he lauded the virtues of "courage, insight, sympathy, solitude" (BGE 284). While in *Daybreak*, his most positive work, in a section on "cardinal virtues" he listed the "*good four*: —Honest towards ourselves and whoever else is a friend to us: *brave* towards the enemy; *magnanimous* towards the defeated; *polite*—always" (D 556). In the end, Nietzsche wants us to return to the values of Aristotle's *megalopsychos*, the "great-souled man". Having conquered rancour, resentment and envy Nietzsche's Superman overflows with benevolence: "It is richness in personality, abundance in oneself, over-flowing and bestowing, instinctive good health and affirmation of oneself, that produce great sacrifice and great love" (WTP 388).

7

Beware the
compassionate
Crying in public

There was a time, before the widespread public grief following the death of Diana, Princess of Wales, in 1997, or before
Paul Gascoigne's tears at the 1990 World Cup in Italy, when
emoting in public and ostentatious shows of compassion
were not the done thing. In 1872 Charles Darwin noted that
"savages weep copiously from very slight causes" while the
English "rarely cry, except under the pressure of the acutest
grief" (Darwin, 1989, p. 117). We have returned to pre-
Victorian ways, where public tears are deemed the norm
and indeed praiseworthy. Olympic athletes routinely break
into tears upon triumph or defeat, as do talent show con-
testants, win or lose, having endured an "emotional roller-
coaster". People have no shame about revealing on television their troubled personal lives before Piers Morgan (if
you are famous) or Jeremy Kyle (if you aren't). Public
emotion is deemed good often because it shows compassion.
"Where are your tears, Ma'am?", asked the tearful crowd
after Diana's death, puzzled that the Queen wasn't joining in
the sob-fest.

Nietzsche thought even his 19th-century contemporaries
had become too lachrymose, groaning how "one lets much
suffering be seen and heard that one formerly bore and hid"
(WTP 60). In *Daybreak* he asked: "What does it indicate that

our culture is not merely tolerant of expressions of pain, of tears, complaints, reproaches, gestures of rage or of humiliation, but approves of them and counts them among the nobler inescapables? Would those philosophers of antiquity perhaps regard us one and all as belonging to the rabble" (D 157).

Nietzsche disliked public displays of emotion because he saw them as a manifestation of the herd mentality. He also believed that pity was contagious, fostering a culture of morbid misery-worship that would eventually look upon happiness with suspicion. Pity was "a squandering of feeling, a parasite harmful to moral health... If one does good merely out of pity, it is oneself one really does good to, and not the other... The suffering of others infects us, pity is an infection" (WTP 368).

He scorned the herd mentality because he saw in it the emotion of *ressentiment* in action, the dark forces of the Will to Power in action. *Ressentiment* is hostility directed at that which one identifies as the cause of one's frustration, of assigning a target of blame for one's frustration, or as Camus put it: "the evil secretion, in a sealed vessel, of prolonged incompetence" (Camus, 2000, p. 5).

Ressentiment is the driving force behind the egalitarianism expressed in Christianity and socialism, which demonises the rich and successful by making pride and wealth sinful. Compassion, morality, egalitarianism and mob rule are all intimately entwined because each is driven by the vengeful desire to exert power over others. Nietzsche used the French word deliberately. In his own language, *Antipathie, Widerstreben* or *Abneigung* all correspond to rancour but none has that specific sense of resentment from a position of inferiority that the French word has. The word conveys a more profound feeling of resentment than the French everyday equivalent *rancoeur* — much in the way *ennui* means something more intense than mere "boredom".

Egalitarianism is but a creed designed to stop others succeeding: "one speaks of '*equal rights*' — that is, as long as one has not yet gained superiority one wants to prevent one's competitors from growing in power" (WTP 86). Egalitarianism and resentment are human sensations in a vicious circle. *Ressentiment* created egalitarianism which in turn generated but more envy and rancour. If you are taught to love your neighbour as yourself you end up hating him. "*The compassionate Christian.* — The reverse side of Christian compassion for the suffering of one's neighbour is a profound suspicion of all the joys of one's neighbour, of his joy in all that he wants to do and can" (D 80), he wrote in *Daybreak*.

A creed founded upon envy must remain rooted in envy. Christian "love" is created out of the impotence of the have-nots. The egalitarian looking upwards to people higher than him becomes envious; looking downwards he gloats. The insincerity of Christian "love", Nietzsche wrote, manifests itself in pity and compassion, which are but masks for taking pleasure in the misfortunes of others. "*What is 'elevating' in our neighbour's misfortune*. He has experienced a misfortune, and now the 'compassionate' come along and depict his misfortune for him in detail — at length they go away content and elevated: they have gloated over the unfortunate man's distress and over their own and passed a pleasant afternoon" (D 224).

Hence compassion and displays of pity are intrinsically self-centred and infantile. They are experienced in order to make a person feel pleasure. As he wrote in *Human, All Too Human*, "observe how children weep and cry, so that they will be pitied, how they wait for the moment when their condition will be noticed... When expressions of pity make the unfortunate man aware of this superiority, he gets a kind of pleasure from it; his self-image revives. Thus the thirst for self-pity is a thirst for self-enjoyment, and at the expense of one's fellow man" (HATH 50).

This verdict could have been applied to the Band Aid and Live Aid episode of 1984–85, in which millions of well-meaning people in the West, by wanting to appear to be doing good, donated money that ended up being delivered into the hands of African kleptocrats who used it to buy weapons. "For the stupidity of the good is unfathomable", he wrote in *Zarathustra*: "the harm the good do is the most harmful harm" (pp. 205, 229). It could still be applied to aid to the Third World in general, which some argue keeps the poor in their place. It is no excuse that the "do-gooder", a pejorative term once common in Britain, says he means well. "Alas, where in the world have there been greater follies than with the compassionate? And what in the world has caused more suffering than the follies of the compassionate?" (TSZ OTC).

Nietzsche would say the same about those who give money to beggars, alms that might be spent on drugs and alcohol, that will ensure they remain homeless, and makes only the donor feel better (Nietzsche was aware to the acute dilemma faced by the sight of beggars: "Beggars, however, should be entirely abolished! Truly, it is annoying to give to them and annoying not to give to them" (TSZ 113)). Giving money both allows the donor to assert his superiority and reinforce the submissive status of the recipient. Another vicious circle ensues, as this induces more *ressentiment*. "I'm not a charity case" is the legitimate cry of those who recognise how belittling it is to live a life of dependence.

Charity usually breeds resentment, among those giving it and those receiving it. Nietzsche wouldn't have been surprised at those areas of Wales that voted to leave the EU in 2016, areas that bear large signs declaring that they have been recipients of EU largesse. Who would want to be part of an organisation that reminded you every day of your humiliating state of dependency? As Nietzsche wrote in *Human, All Too Human*: "It shows a complete lack of noble character when someone prefers to live in dependence, at the expense of others, in order not to work at any cost, and usually with a secret bitterness towards those on whom he is dependent" (HATH 356).

Nietzsche believed that Christian morality is a pious fraud, and that behind every noble gesture there lay a desire to assert power, from which one ultimately derived pleasure. We may see the self-exalting of the self in today's culture, from confessional television to selfies on Instagram, as a result of the crisis in authority which Nietzsche identified. With the death of God, followed by the withering of ties to the nation or class and the emergence of identity politics, the reference point of authority for individuals in our lifetimes has gradually retreated towards the self.

The late 20th century saw the age of the narcissism develop in two stages. First there was the social revolution of the 1960s, and the championing of individual choice, self-determination and liberation. Then there came the economic revolution of the 1980s and the emergence of market-place individualism. It's a toxic combination made all the more acute by the third, digital, revolution of the 2000s, which has been an enabler of this culture of narcissism. It's no wonder, to quote the subtitle of the memoirs of the *Sunday Times* and *Spectator* columnist Rod Liddle, that we have become "greedy, narcissistic and unhappy".

As Liddle writes: "It is no coincidence that this rapid erosion of deference to an omnipotent, unseen other has occurred in tandem with the growth of institutionalised self-obsession, self-pity and public emoting. If there is no unseen other to bow down before, we bow down instead before ourselves... 'I am all that matters, and my petty vicissitudes, my miseries, will no longer be internalised but shared, at interminable length, with a grateful world'." Liddle concludes with a quite Nietzschean flourish: "Keep it to yourself, your heroin addiction or your anorexia or your alcoholism or your mid-life crisis, you mug;... in the meantime, struggle on with fortitude and reserve" (Liddle, 2014, p. 18).

Essentially, Nietzsche calls for dignity, reserve and resilience: the values of nobility and transcendence from petty, childish, self-destructive feelings. *Ressentiment* and self-pity lead you to a dead end: "nothing burns one up quicker than the affects of *ressentiment*. Vexation, morbid susceptibility, incapacity for revenge, the desire, the thirst for revenge" (EH WIASW.6).

8

Equality to the equal, inequality to the unequal
Dumbing down

Although Nietzsche asserted that all should achieve their potential, he didn't believe that everyone had the same potential. Mob values would have to be retained by the mob, while the "higher types" would employ self-mastery to rise above them. "'Equality for equals, inequality for unequals' — *that* would be the true voice of justice: and, what follows from it, 'Never make equal what is unequal'" (TOTI EUM 48). In this he believed in a nobility that would rule lower types. That doesn't sound appealing to us today. Neither did he clarify how this society with a new nobility would come about or be arranged. Systematic thinking was not his forte and the fineries of political theory never his thing. Nietzsche preferred instead to talk in abstract terms, about "forces" and "spirits". Yet there are many who would agree with Nietzsche that egalitarianism is debilitating when it becomes so doctrinal that it ends up levelling everyone down rather up. This is why he decried Christianity and socialism, for casting suspicion on those who wanted to ascend higher and to be better.

There has for some time been the complaint that our culture has "dumbed down", and has become more vulgar and demotic. This cry is a reaction to base egalitarianism that has held sway since the 1960s. This philosophy remains tenacious. To accuse someone of "elitism" is a grievous charge today, in a culture in which seemingly so many regard themselves in opposition to a nebulous "Establishment". Today, people who are middle class, male, straight or white are rebuked online with the refrain to "check your privilege", i.e. not to voice an opinion unless you have been a victim of sorts. Nietzsche would have regarded this as the logical result of promoting egalitarianism, which, in seeking to erase life's injustices, ends up promoting mediocrity in its race to the bottom. Egalitarianism without deference or authority will always generate resentment of those in power, and lead to the belittlement of those who pursue excellence.

Nietzsche believed that a healthy society is one in which there prevails an aspirational force that pulls us towards something higher and better. "All individuals can be viewed in terms of whether they represent the ascending or the descending line of life" (TOTI EUM 33). Those of the ascending line harness instinct and seek to maximise their innate capacity. They face suffering with neither remorse nor resentment. When this ascensional force loses its force, it is no longer venerated, causing it to lose its momentum further, to stagnate and then becomes descensional. When, besieged by egalitarianism, authority begins to doubt itself or fear unpopularity or accusations of "unfairness", it starts to lose its power and allure. "Traditional" values and authority crumbles, and it does so when it loses confidence in itself. Our culture has become "dumbed down" because "elitist" has become a term of abuse, a word pertaining to experts or to those with higher and better knowledge.

Today "non-judgementalism" rules. Culture is dumbed down when those in authority stop believing in their own authority, and a race to the bottom ensues. In academia, especially, "a trend has emerged whereby some within universities see the Enlightenment origins of academic freedom as tainting it with an elitism that serves only to further the interests of already dominant voices" (Williams, 2016, p. 12). This notion that we should "check our privilege" is the product of the idea that knowledge is inextricably rendered subjective on account of who is holding it. Since the 1960s there has been a cultural assault on deference, on the idea that some knowledge can be objectively attained, and that this knowledge is superior and valid to other knowledge that has not earned its merit.

Authority that doubts itself will crumble and end up invalidating itself. A doubting authority becomes its own assassin. Secondary school children recognise this phenomenon instinctively. It's "the trendy teacher syndrome", whereby that new master who now wants to be your friend, to call him by his first name, to be your equal. From the outset he is first ridiculed and then held in contempt by his teachers, precisely on account of not exerting his authority. The end result is that his pupils will not pay attention, not learn and not fulfil their potential.

Once, when pupils were punished at school, parents would always take the side of the teachers. Now they instinctively side with their children. One time, if a child was disciplined, even the school's head would automatically back his or her teacher. Not so any more. Now, even pupils are consulted about which teachers their school should employ, breeding further contempt.

Nietzsche would recognise the consequences of the lack of confidence among those in ostensible and erstwhile positions of authority. The Church of England has seen its numbers dwindle over the decade, a decline hastened precisely by its doubting, "inclusive" members in the pulpit. Contrast its fate that to the growth of muscular Evangelical churches or Islam, from faiths that dare to say they know the truth and you don't, faiths that exert their Will to Power.

Witness, too, modern art's crisis of authority. Installation art is lauded for being "challenging", with its aesthetic merit of secondary importance. "Edginess" or transgressiveness, as opposed to excellence or beauty, is deemed the main criterion of worth. Indeed, installation art's very ugliness is its driving force, in direct opposition to the traditional, and by implication "elitist", notion of "beauty". Tracey Emin's installation art is lauded because it has no meaning beyond reference to its creator. It's all about the subjective her.

Books are derided on account of being penned by dead, white males. The BBC, desperate not too appear too "high-brow", is decried by demotic, egalitarian Right-wing news-papers for "not giving value for money". As for tabloid newspapers themselves: what could be a more vivid example of a dumbed down culture than their emergence in the past fifty years? The working class no longer aspires to be as educated as their grandparents did. Those who say they prefer going to the opera than football are liable to the charge of being a snob.

Nietzsche's valorisation of the principle of ennoblement was partly inspired by the commercialised age in which he lived, one in which he thought everything was debased to its lowest level in the name of profit. Although he was a keen newspaper reader as youth, Nietzsche essentially resented the press for encouraging frivolity and gossip: "Just look at these superfluous people!… they vomit their bile and call it a newspaper" (TSZ OTNI). Newspapers epitomised a shallow, dumbed down culture, as he elaborated in *Human, All Too Human*: "The fools of modern culture. Our feuilleton writers are like medieval court fools: it is the same category of people. Half-rational, witty, excessive, silly, they are some-times there only to soften the atmosphere of pathos with whimsy and chatter, and to drown out with their shouting the all too ponderous, solemn tintinnabulation of great events" (HATH 194). He advised that "scientific men should not become journalists. We mistrust any form of culture that tolerates newspaper reading or writing" (WTP 132).

The paradox is that Friedrich Nietzsche, the man who had opinions on everything, the one who wrote with such entertaining ferocity, would have made for a first-rate newspaper columnist. A-Level grade inflation, diversity quotas in the workplace, wealthy actors speaking out for Syrian refugees, trendy vicars, *Celebrity Big Brother,* Brexiteers against the elites: such topics would have been grist to his mill. His bellyaching about tenured academics, what with their security and safe salaries, marks him out as a classic freelance writer.

Not only was Nietzsche a gifted and entertaining writer who relished paradoxes and jokes, he had a gift for puns, rhyming and wordplay — the essence of tabloid newspapers. This is lost on those of us who read his works in English. For instance, in *Human All Too Human* we read that "leisure and idleness are a noble thing". In the original this is: *"Es ist aber ein edel Ding um Muße und Müßiggehen"* (HATH 285). Elsewhere: *"Pity more intense than suffering"* is *"Mitleiden stärker als Leiden"* (HATH 46). Similarly, "self-cancellation" and "self-overcoming" in the *Genealogy* are *Selbstaufhebung* and *Selbstüberwindung* respectively (GOM 3.27). *"Fehlschluss, Fehlschuss"*, he had penned in *Die fröhliche Wissenschaft*, which in *The Joyous Science* becomes: *"Bad reasoning, bad shot"* (TJS 227). He even extended his wordplay to Latin: *"pulchrum est paucorum hominum"* — "beauty belongs to the few" (WTP 783).

There is a terrible irony about Nietzsche and cultural relativism, about our timidity or inability to discriminate between better and worse. Nietzsche not only foresaw it, he helped to bring it about — as Allan Bloom and many others have pointed out. Forming his influential theories in the 1960s, Foucault, perhaps the godfather of 20th-century postmodernist relativism, was deeply indebted to Nietzsche's writings on subjectivity and meaning. The postmodernist notion that truth is relative has since seeped down from academia through schools and into wider society. Few who enrol in humanities courses at university will be unfamiliar with Nietzsche's quote that "Truth is a mobile army of metaphors, metonyms, anthropomorphisms, in short a sum of human relations which have been subjected to poetic and rhetorical intensification, translation and decoration [...]; truths are illusions of which we have forgotten that they are illusions, metaphors which have become worn by frequent use and have lost all sensuous vigour" (from the essay "On Truth and Lies in a Nonmoral Sense", 1873).

Yet the idea that truth is subjective needn't sound so alarming. We readily accept that value judgements can be subjective within certain parameters. We have always tacitly accepted the notion in our legal system. Different judges have different ways of interpreting the law, and they gain different reputations accordingly—for being harsh or lenient. In law we also have character witnesses, that is to say, we accept that veracity of something is dependent on who says it. The same goes for football referees, some of whom are more draconian than others, yet each interprets the laws of the game legitimately. And who says a statement does affect its veracity. Who would you accept advice from on the matter of the link between cigarettes and cancer: representative of a tobacco firm or a doctor?

We also accept that all truth is subject to change over time, that truths are contingently held. Otherwise there would be no progress in science. Scientific theories have to compete with each other to gain legitimacy, and scientific knowledge changes as its progresses. Copernicus was right, but so was Galileo after him, and Newton and Einstein following on. Plate tectonics only achieved respectability in the postwar era. Even Nietzsche conceded that contingent, imprecise truths were useful for our everyday lives, writing: "One should not understand this compulsion to construct concepts, species, forms, purposes, laws... as if they enable us to fix the *real world*; but as a compulsion to arrange a world for ourselves in which our existence is made possible:—we thereby create a world which is calculable, simplified, comprehensible, etc., for us" (WTP 521).

We also tacitly accept, or believe, that moral values change and indeed improve over time. As Nietzsche himself observed: "The learned judge correctly that people of all ages have believed they *know* what is good and evil, praise- and blameworthy. But it is a prejudice of the learned that *we now know* better" (D 2). We pride ourselves on the fact that slavery is no longer deemed acceptable or normal as it once was or that women can vote and should have equal rights. In living memory attitudes towards homosexuality have changed remarkably. When it comes to the contemporary morals, we are reluctant to call ourselves moral relativists— that one man's values today are different and equally valid as the next's—but we are temporal moral relativists. We believe values change over time and that this is a good and necessary thing. No doubt, Britons of the future will find fault with the UK of 2016 and they will look down upon us for being "backward".

We shouldn't confuse relativism with perspectivism, either. Consider four people in each corner in Trafalgar Square. Each points to the centre. One says: "That is Nelson's Column." Another says: "*Das ist Nelson-Säule.*" A third: "*Questo è Colonna di Nelson.*" All three are saying different words from different perspectives and each utters a state- ment which is equally true and valid. But what of a fourth spectator who says: "*Telle est la Tour Eiffel*"? By consensus, we can agree that this statement isn't true.

Not all statements are equal on the say-so of those uttering it, but perspectives can be different and equally valid. A road map of Britain, a geological map of Britain and a political map of Britain all tell you very different things about a country and all are equally valid. All best-selling books about Nietzsche that you will come across in your local book store tell you different things about the man from a different perspective, but they each have a validity of their own. Contrarily, not everything you read about Nietzsche on the internet or might hear in the pub is equally valid. Truth and validity has to be fought over and earned.

We defer to Nietzschean scholars in print and to maps made by the AA or Collins because we still believe others have higher knowledge than ourselves. We are tacitly happy to believe in elites, or defer to authority, when it comes to pragmatic matters. We wouldn't entrust anyone to fly a passenger jet or perform brain surgery on us. In our leisure we believe in hierarchy, as manifest in football league tables and divisions, tennis rankings and Olympic medal tables. We are not as egalitarian as we like to think we are. True, blanket relativism, often attributed to and blamed on Nietzsche, has not triumphed. Egalitarianism, which Nietzsche, rather, abhorred, has neither come to fruition in our culture. Of relativism: conservatives only fear it is with us. Of egalitarianism: the liberal-Left only gives lip service to it.

Nietzsche wrote that "any species of men (a people or a race) seems to be doomed as soon as it becomes tolerant, grants equal rights, and no longer desires to become a master" (WTP 354). Perhaps these words are a little extreme for our palate, but there is something in his sentiments that rings true, that a culture that has lost its confidence or its capacity to tell better from worse has problems. Nietzsche would denounce top-down egalitarianism in the work-place, quotas based on ethnicity, gender or class. He would decry the annual improvements in A-Level results, perceiving this the consequence of making them easier. He wouldn't ask for quotas in universities for children from state schools; he would urge state schools to outperform their private counterparts instead. His message: surpass others and go beyond even yourself. Egalitarianism can drag everyone down. Nietzsche instead asked that we become faster, stronger, higher.

9

Leisure and idleness are a noble thing
Digital addiction

In May 2016 the veteran broadcaster Joan Bakewell made a speech bemoaning the frenetic pace of life today, that the "world is getting even more frantic". As she told an audience at the Hay Festival: "we live in an urgent world, urgent to get on in life, to get the best job, the best car. It's damaging family life and taking its toll on people's health" by causing an "epidemic of anxiety".

This is a common complaint in our globalised, digital age, and a perception supported by statistics. In his book *The Great Acceleration, How the World is Getting Faster* (2016) Robert Colville relates how in 1960 the average American got between eight and nine hours sleep a night, a figure that had dropped to seven by 2000. From the mid-1990s up to 2006 walking speeds increased by 10 per cent. Attention deficit hyperactivity disorder (ADHD) is the "quintessential modern disease" for an internet culture in which we are bombarded with, frustrated by and addicted to pieces of information. Fear of Missing Out (FOMO) is the typical condition for today's children. Their parents' generation "knew there was a cooler party somewhere", empathises Colville, "but they couldn't see the guest list".

The malaise of digital addiction has been laid out elsewhere by Sherry Turkle in her books *Reclaiming Conversation: The Power of Talk in a Digital Age* and *Alone Together: Why We Expect More from Technology and Less from Each Other.* The technological revolution of the early 21st century, epitomised by the smartphone, is degrading human relations. At the office or at the dinner table colleagues, romantic partners, parents and children can't get each other's undivided attention. Friends at parties spend as much time communicating with virtual friends online as real ones in the room, while in the classroom professors look upon a room of distracted multitaskers.

Internet dating, with its infinite number of choices, has undermined the principle of emotional commitment. There is the unquenchable desire to get "likes" on Facebook and retweets on Twitter. As Rod Liddle observes bluntly: "this inferno, this dismal fugue, surrounds us, jabbers at us, its cretinous tweets burrowing like weird polyester fibres beneath our skin, its imprecations arousing us, everything convincing us to diving in with our own little puked-up gobbet of fucknuts… Half digested shit sprayed from wall to wall forming one single, dark-browned graffito: I am, therefore I must be heard" (Liddle, 2014, p. 214).

The 19th century in which Nietzsche lived was no less convulsive, a time in which the Industrial Revolution came of age. Back then, Nietzsche complained about an increasingly frenetic, globalised world in which gigantic industry was ever-expanding at the expense of creative culture and reflexion. "Overwork, curiosity and sympathy — our *modern vices*" (WTP 73). He believed that industrial capitalism was bad for the soul: "Living in a constant chase after gain compels people to expand their spirit to the point of exhaustion in continual pretence and overreaching and anticipating others" (TJS 329). Elsewhere in *The Joyous Science*, in a passage still resonant, he writes: "Even now one is ashamed of resting, and prolonged reflection almost gives one a bad conscience. One thinks with a watch in one's hand, even as one eats one's midday meal while reading the latest news on the stock market; one lives as if one always 'might miss out on something'" (TJS 329).

Whereas Marx believed that the Industrial Revolution was an inevitable and necessary stage on the path to revolution, and his followers were to decry it for its exploitative nature, Nietzsche disdained modernity from the position of tradition and nobility, albeit an affected one on his behalf. "The born aristocrats of the spirit are not overeager; their creations blossom and fall from the trees on a quiet autumn evening, being neither rashly desired, not hastened on, not supplanted by new things. The wish to create incessantly is vulgar, betraying jealousy, envy, and ambition", he writes in *Human, All Too Human* (210).

Like many in the (actual) landed classes, he regarded capitalists and men on the make as uncouth: "Formerly financiers were looked down upon with honest scorn, even though they were recognised as needful; for it was generally admitted that every society must have its viscera. Now, however, they are the ruling power in the soul of modern humanity, for they constitute the most covetous portion thereof", he wrote in 1875. "In former times people were warned especially against taking the day or the moment too seriously; the nil admirari was recommended and the care of things eternal. How there is but one kind of seriousness left in the modern mind, and it is limited to the news brought by the newspaper and the telegraph. Improve each shining hour, turn it in to some account and judge it as quickly as possible!" He concludes by berating the "omnipresence of disgusting and insatiable cupidity, and spying inquisitiveness become universal" (UM 4 vi).

While Nietzsche agreed with Marx about industrial capitalism's alienating effect, Nietzsche did not believe in "the glorification of 'work', in the unwearied talk of the 'blessing of work'" (D 173). Work was a dehumanising narcotic which "gnaws at and poisons life... with this inhuman clockwork and mechanism, with the '*im*person-ality' of the worker" (EH THE.1). Capitalist modernity and work stops us thinking, it prevents us from being miserable and all too human. "For it uses up an extraordinary amount of nervous energy, which is thus denied to reflection, brood-ing, dreaming, worrying, loving, hating; it sets a small goal always in sight and guarantees easy and regular satis-factions" (D 173).

This disdain of capitalism and industry explains why Nietzsche deplores the English so vehemently and cease-lessly, a people he regarded as shallow, a nation that even turned the values of the market-place into a philosophy: utilitarianism, with its technocratic talk of maximising pleasure and minimising pain. "They are a modest and thoroughly mediocre species of man, these English utili-tarians" (BGE 228). He believed: "Utility and pleasure are *slave theories* of life: the 'blessing of work' is the self-glorification of slaves — Incapacity for *otium* [leisure]' (WTP 681).

Nietzsche looked down on the Englishman on account of his life-negating, mindless industriousness. "The Man *who has become free* — and how much more the *mind* that has become free — spurns the contemptible sort of well-being dreamed of by shopkeepers, Christians, cows, women, Englishmen and other democrats. The free man is a *warrior*" (one's of Nietzsche's most unappealing aspects was his misogyny) (TOTI EOAUM 38). Nietzsche speaks of the "profound averageness" (BGE 253) of the Englishman and "his lack of music" (BGE 252), a common observation on the continent, especially before Elgar and Vaughan Williams. Nietzsche even went as far to compose an ode to the "pon-derous" and "boring" Englishman:

> Hail, continual plodders, hail!
> Lengthen out the tedious tale
> Pedant still in head and knee
> Dull, of humour not a trace

Permanently commonplace
Sans ge'nie et sans espirit. (BGE 228)

All this is harsh stuff to the ears of an Englander, you might say, but who could argue with this observation in *Beyond Good and Evil*: "The industrious races find leisure very hard to endure: it was a masterpiece of *English* instinct to make Sunday so extremely holy and boring that the English unconsciously long again for their week- and working-days —as a kind of cleverly devised and cleverly intercalated *fast*" (BGE 189). Yet Nietzsche wouldn't get excited about campaigns to liberalise Sunday trading laws; rather, he would urge instead that there be less soul-sapping industry done the entire week.

We can conclude that Nietzsche is no neophile. It is highly doubtful that today he would put up a selfie on social media. Instead, he would recoil at the attention-seeking vanity of Facebook or Instagram: "you are laughable to me, you men of the present! And especially when you are amazed at yourself!" (TSZ OTLOC). And as for the opinionated timewasters forever on Twitter: "O you poor devils in the great cities of the world, you gifted young men tormented by ambition who consider it your duty to pass some comment on everything that happens!… always on the lookout for the moment when they can put their word in, lose all genuine productivity!" (D 177).

He would not be one to "like" or "♥" your post. Even real-life friendship went against his philosophy of struggle. "The man of knowledge must be able not only to love his enemies but also to hate his friends" (TSZ 1 22), he wrote, a maxim applicable to the poisonous mood found on social media in Britain during and after the June 2016 vote to leave the EU.

Nietzsche wouldn't be bothered about amazing photos of himself not getting "liked", descend into despondency because everyone else online is seemingly having a better time than him. He would probably urge instead that other people "hate" photos we put up of ourselves. He would rise above the misery-inducing clamour of social media, with the fake, "perfect" lives presented on it. In our frenzied hyper-connected world, he would seek solace in the mountains alone, away from the Instagrammers: "The solitary, however, have their enjoyment or their torment of a thing in silence, they hate a clever and glittering display of their innermost problems as they hate to see their beloved too carefully dressed" (D 524). As he advised: "If one stays silent for a year one unlearns chattering and learns to speak" (D 347).

10

The Will to Power
The politics of envy

If Nietzsche abhorred vulgarian capitalism for its dehumanising effects, he had little time for the political Left. It could
be said that the only people he loathed as much as Christians
were socialists, but that would be to miss the point. He made
no fundamental distinction between the two. He saw
socialism as an offshoot of Christianity, of its notion in the
equality of man, itself the product of envy and avarice. "You
preachers of equality, thus from you the tyrant-madness of
impotence cries for 'equality'; thus your most secret tyrant-
appetite disguises itself in words of virtue. Soured self-
conceit, repressed envy... they burst from you as a flame
and madness of revenge" (TSZ OTT). Zarathustra's words
are not directed here against any group in particular, as
Nietzsche made little distinction between secular or religious
egalitarians.

A feeling of *ressentiment* is inherent to egalitarian ideologies, which emerge out of feelings of envy: "to demand
equality of rights, as to the socialists of the subjugated caste,
never results from justice but rather covetousness. If one
shows the beast bloody pieces of meat close by, and then
draw them away again until finally it roars, do you think
this roar means justice?" (HATH 451). Because envy is the
motive behind egalitarianism, a society in which its spirit
dominates is destined to resent and suppress those individuals who want to be stronger or go higher. "*The collective*

degeneration of man down to that which the socialist dolts and
blockheads today see as their 'man of the future' — as their
ideal! — this degeneration and diminution of man to the
perfect herd animal (or, as they say, to the man of the 'free
society'), this animalization of man to the pygmy animal of
equal rights and equal pretensions is possible, there is no
doubt about that! He who has once thought this possibility
through to the end knows one more kind of disgust than
other men do" (BGE 203). Socialism brings everyone down
to the basest level because it cannot tolerate the individual
who seeks to go beyond, to stray from the tribe. Cultures
ruled by a resentful, envious multitude will ostracise or
persecute exceptional men.

It's an irony that some of Nietzsche's earliest followers
were socialists, as it is that some of them were anarchists.
Nietzsche's rhetoric may sound destructive and his writings
may have an anarchistic resonance, but he had little time for
Left-wing revolutionaries or anti-state libertarian extremists.
Both were resentful types. "The Christian and the anarchist",
he wrote in *The Antichrist*, "both *bloodsuckers*, both with the
instinct of *deadly hatred* towards everything that stands erect,
that towers grandly up, that possesses duration, that
promises a future" (TAC 192). Nietzsche was no more an
anarchist than he was an atheist. He was concerned with
liberating oneself from all ideologies and conventional
morality.

In *Human, All Too Human*, Nietzsche assails Jean Jacques
Rousseau, the man who popularised the revolutionary
notion that "man is born free but is everywhere in chains"
and the noble savagery at the heart of socialism: "There are
political and social visionaries who hotly and eloquently
demand the overthrow of all orders, in the belief that
proudest temple of fair humanity would then immediately
rise up on its own. In these dangerous dreams, there is still
the echo of Rousseau's superstition, which believes in a
wondrous, innate, but, as it were, *repressed* goodness of
human nature, and attributes all the blame for that

repression to the institutions of culture, in society, state and education. Unfortunately, we know from historical experience that every such overthrow once more resurrects the wildest energies, the long since buried horrors and extravagances of most distant times" (HATH 463).

Man is inherently driven by the Will to Power, hence all morality systems have their foundation on violence, actual or threatened. Nietzsche observed that while "socialists prove that the distribution of wealth in present-day society is the consequence of countless injustices and atrocities", they fail at the same time to comprehend or acknowledge that "the entire past of the old culture was erected upon force, slavery, deception, error... we, the heirs and inheritors of all these past things" (HATH 452).

Like Edmund Burke before, or George Orwell after, Nietzsche recognised the inherent dangers of socialism and humanism. Those who seize power become intoxicated by it, especially if they mean well. Burke, in *Reflections on the Revolution in France*, and Orwell, in *Animal Farm*, recognised that revolutions based on egalitarian principles inevitably lead to despotism. This is because human beings are not inherently good people merely corrupted by culture or bad environment—as socialist utopians would have us believe.

To believe in the inherent goodness of man is ultimately to let evil triumph because it allows the worst, most cunning and lustful types to rise to power. The naive, innocent Left underplays or ignores the dark side of the Will to Power. Nietzsche foresaw that the death of God would presage a great calamity if humanism and the worship of man were to take its place. After God, after morality, what next?, he asked. His answer: "Intoxication as music; intoxication as cruelty in the tragic enjoyment of the destruction of the noblest; intoxication as blind enthusiasm for single human beings" (WTP 27).

Nietzsche's dislike of socialists and humanitarians goes to explain his revulsion towards anti-Semitism. In *On the Genealogy of Morals* he spoke how this "ressentiment... this plant now blooms most beautifully among anarchists and anti-Semites" (GOM 2.11). Anti-Semitism was the emotion held by those who resented the success of others, for whom "Someone must be to blame for the fact that I do not feel well" (GOM 3.15). Socialists and egalitarians and those driven by envy hated the Jews on account of "their energy and higher intelligence, their capital spirit and will, which accumulated from generation to generation in the long school of their suffering, must predominate to a degree that awakens envy and hatred… scapegoats for every possible public and private misfortune" (HATH 475).

Therefore it was no surprise that anti-Semitism became the guiding credo of National Socialism in Germany, the ultimate expression of *ressentiment* as led by a failed artist and fourth-rate author. "Whoever is dissatisfied with himself is continually ready for revenge, and we others will be his victims, if only by having to endure his ugly site. For the sight of what is ugly makes one bad and gloomy" (TJS 290). It's no surprise either that anti-Semitism has become commonplace in the Left in Britain today, both in student union politics and grown-up politics. Student activists forever berating all that is white and male, scolding us to "check our privilege": they brim with *ressentiment*, too. Resentment and anti-Semitism will always be found side-by-side, especially on the Left, where the politics of envy continually fester.

Nietzsche recognised that the underling intoxicated by the desire for power and revenge will eventually become the ruthless overling. All revolutions against tyranny throw up new tyrants once power is achieved. "Socialism is the visionary younger brother of an almost decrepit despotism, whose heir it wants to be. Thus its efforts are reactionary in the deepest sense. For it desires a wealth of executive power, as only despotism had it" (HATH 473), he wrote, stating his belief that socialism leads to autocracy. As Joanna Williams notes of erstwhile radical students today: "It is notable that many trends that today appear to restrict academic freedom or enforce the culture of conformity in universities began as progressive attempts to expand knowledge into new areas and utilize new methods... Today such radical ideas often tend to shape the pursuit of knowledge in a more partial and stifling direction than the traditional approaches they critiqued" (Williams, 2016, p. 7).

Nietzsche saw how perilous the creeping power of the state worship would be: "The state is the coldest of all cold monsters. Coldly it lies, too; and this lie creeps from its mouth: 'I, the state, am the people'" (TSZ OTNI). On the basis of writings such as this, Nietzsche has been recruited by many libertarians or anti-statist free-marketeers on the Right. But he was no Thatcherite, or early advocate of Reagonomics. He would have baulked at the servile worship of the forces of the free market, as often becomes the destiny of capitalist fundamentalists. Nietzsche belongs neither to the Left nor Right, because he wouldn't want to be cajoled into any political philosophy. Egalitarianism, state-worship and neoliberalism: all are a denial of the individual will, of outsourcing one's creative energy to some other force, some ideology. All "-isms" are the manifestation of lazy, herd-thinking. *"Envy and sloth in different directions.* The two opposing parties, the socialistic and the nationalistic", he concluded, "deserve one another; in both of them, envy and laziness are the moving powers. In the one camp, people want to work as little as possible with their hands; in the other, as little as possible with their heads" (HATH 480).

Conclusion
Beyond Good and Evil

Friedrich Nietzsche has always been regarded and feared as a dangerous thinker. Therein lies the reason for his perpetual appeal, and therein lies the reason why his name will forever be defamed. It was not just his association with dangerous political ideas that renders him a figure of lurid fascination, but his explicitly stated immorality. It's this professed immorality, or at least amorality and deep cynicism of conventional morality, that rightly alarms people. Imagine a world in which everyone sought to realise the dark side of their own Will to Power, create their own values, in which everyone sought to overcome everyone else. "This is what *I* am; this is what *I* want:—*you* can go hell!' (WTP 350), as Nietzsche once put it. Imagine if we all carried on like Kevin Kline's character Otto in the film *A Fish Called Wanda* (1988), one of the best-known fictional Nietzsche disciples—a shallow and poisonous oaf who eats fish alive and shoves chips up people's noses.

A world in which everyone took it upon themselves to be their own Superman might be a libertine nightmare, a ferocious, ultra-Darwinian prospect. The result would not be a liberated society of "free spirits" but one ultimately ruled by the strongest. Might would make right. Power-worship begets violence. As Camus wrote: "Unlimited liberty of desire implies the negation of others and the suppression of pity" (Camus, 2000, p. 20).

Nietzsche's sometimes sorry reputation is in many ways deserved. Nietzsche called for the "re-evaluation of all values", yet he never specified what these were to be, or how they would be established. Nietzsche was vague on the actual details of his Superman, and he had little concrete and constructive to say politically. As he himself admitted, "I have tried to deny everything: oh tearing down is easy, but building up!" (cited in Jaspers, 1961, p. 10). Nietzsche's vague and violent language was irresponsible. And regimes that have sought to create society afresh, having fashioned new morals from the start, which take *"joy even in destruction"* (EH TSZ 8) have invariably been the most cruel and totalitarian. Nietzsche's revolutionary calls to start again after having destroyed that which has been with us can't help bring to mind the Khmer Rouge's "Year Zero".

It is not entirely clear, either, that he took his own doctrine of Eternal Recurrence — the idea that we will all live our lives over again in perpetuity — that seriously even himself. He only mentions it a few times and only fleetingly. It was probably more of a recommendation. As Scruton puts it: "Nietzsche's exuberant invocation of 'eternal recurrence' is not a metaphysical thesis. It is an exhortation to live as if everything eternally recurs" (Scruton, 2015, p. 184). It is perhaps no coincidence that it appears substantially in notes he didn't commit to a book himself, referring to the idea as "my consolation" (WTP 1065). The notion reeks too much of Schopenhauerian metaphysical fancy which Nietzsche later and sustainedly rebutted. Soloman felt confident to "dismiss the thesis out of hand as a combination of outdated physics and faulty mathematics" (Soloman, 2003, p. 14). His "Eternal Recurrence" ultimately negates human agency, the very essence of Nietzsche's writings, which he emphasised in abundance.

His views, too, on women are repugnant to the modern reader: "Woman has so much reason for shame; in women there is concealed so much pedanticism, superficiality, schoolmarmishness, petty presumption, petty unbrideldness and petty immodesty", he wrote in *Beyond Good and Evil* (232). His misogyny may stem from having grown up in a household full of women without a father. He may have picked it up from Schopenhauer, a first-rate woman hater. It could have been the result of contracting syphilis from a prostitute, having visited a brothel as a youth—the syphilis that most likely was the principal source of his madness.

All this might have been compounded by being rebuffed by a young, beautiful Russian intellectual of French origin, Lou Salomé, to whom he proposed to twice in the early 1880s. This left him devastated. Thereafter his contact with women was minimal. Women in general, concludes Hollingdale, were "for Nietzsche something strange, mystifying and, above all, tempting; if there is one persistent refrain running through his writings about them, it is that they lure men from the path of greatness, and spoil and corrupt them"(Hollingdale, 1985, p. 151).

Nietzsche had no children, which probably contributed to his arrested development and his cavalier attitudes towards morality. Parents, rather than footloose singletons, are far more attached to the idea of self-evident morality and the need to instil it in others. Parents are less attracted to the idea of perpetual change and more concerned in creating a stable and safe environment. Parents aren't keen on their infants "living dangerously", in running out onto busy roads or playing with fire. Parents are less inclined to teach their children that there is no essential difference between telling the truth and telling a lie. Those who have children don't want to go beyond good and evil.

Nietzsche the writer also deserves some ridicule. He could be excessive, slapdash and prone to adolescent exaggeration and overstatement. John Gray regards him as "an inveterately religious thinker, whose incessant attacks on Christian beliefs and values attest to the fact that he could never shake them off" (Gray, 2003, p. 45), and he did have the manner of a fundamentalist, monomaniac bore at times.

As Figgis put it so aptly in 1917: "Nietzsche is a good tonic, but a bad food" (Figgis, 1917, p. 290).

Perhaps, too, Nietzsche was the true godfather of cultural relativism. His words live on in infamy: "there are *no eternal facts*, nor are there any absolute truths" (HATH 2). And such relativism is ultimately self-defeating and self-contradictory. To assert that objective truth is a fiction itself is an objective statement. But this shouldn't negate the idea that facts can be temporary or that truths can be *practical* — or that some are better and more useful than others. Not all opinions are equal: some assert themselves to be more powerful. This would accord with the Enlightenment notion that truths were contingent: true until the time came when they could be falsified.

As for his immorality embodied in the lines "There are no moral phenomena at all, only a moral interpretation of phenomena" (BGE 108), what he was foremost concerned with here was to expose the immorality of Christian morals, not to negate the whole notion of morality itself. "Though he called himself an immoralist, he was really a moralist who exposed the self-deceptions inherent in previous moral-izing" (Hayman, 1980, pp. 355–6). Nietzsche believed in the usefulness of morality, not any claims to transcendental truth. He didn't believe morals had any values beyond themselves, and weren't delivered by a higher power. Christianity's assertion that its morality embodies "good" is a deception and a mendacity. Christian morals were a manifestation of a tribal survival instinct, a mutual assistance scheme with baseless appeals to a punitive God. "Morality as the work of immorality. For moral values to gain dominion they must be assisted by lots of immoral forces and affects" (WTP 266).

While Nietzsche has shortcomings, in this tumultuous age of religious fundamentalism and populist rage he remains relevant. He might support the new populists who rail against the elites, the Donald Trumps, Bernie Sanders and Nigel Farages of the world. But he wouldn't sympathise with their sense of righteousness, or certainly their sense of resentment. He didn't say that 'anything goes', maintaining, rather, that "the libertinage, the principle of *'laisser aller,'* should not be confused with the will to power" (WTP 122).

In our times, Nietzsche is a tonic against rage, certitudes, intolerance and idealism, against both the elites and the herd, against resentment, envy and selfishness. He exhorts us to live with doubt and be free of grand ideas imposed on us by others, to live our lives to the full and without fear. He urged us to question everything, and this includes the libertine and the populist and any whose diseased and selfish exertion of power makes the world a poorer place. He would urge us to strive to better ourselves. "I'm no good at maths", you say. "I'm no good at languages", you insist. Then become the person who is good at maths and who is good at languages.

He didn't want us to go back, but to go forward. This liberation would be both terrifying and jubilant. Ours is the world to make. As he enthused in *The Joyous Science*: "we philosophers and 'free spirits' feel, when we hear the news that 'the old god is dead,' as if a new dawn shone on us; our heart overflows with gratitude, amazement, premonitions, expectation. At long last the horizon appears free to us again, even if it should not be bring; at long last our ships may venture out again, venture out to face any danger; all the daring of the lover of knowledge is permitted again; the sea, our *sea*, likes open again" (TJS 343).

Nietzsche would not set upon settled values. Like the ancient Greek Heraclitus, he saw the world as in a perpetual state of flux, without meaning, without divine sanction, of perpetual struggle, of perpetual doubt. Imagine life as akin to the Myth of Sisyphus, of eternally pushing a boulder up a hill, only to see it fall back down again and again. It takes courage to embrace that fate. But that is life: always struggling. If you don't keep pushing that boulder, it will roll down and destroy you. It takes a brave individual to live without boundaries, rules or prohibitions imposed by others, to break free from ideology, to live dangerously, to question and not answer, to look into the void.

Nietzsche remains invaluable because he demands bravery and honesty and integrity in a digital world of echo-chambers, one evermore divided into conformist and righteous tribes. His Superman does no wrong because he is too busy doing what is right. That is what he ultimately asked: to live life with courage and with sincerity. Through the readings of Nietzsche you can help liberate yourself from ideology and group-think, to be fearless in your thoughts, actions and words. One day you will care not how many likes or retweets you get on social media, or worry what your classmates and peers think of you. You will have the courage to rise above them, go beyond them.

Do not be afraid to be who you are and listen not to what others say, and this includes Friedrich Nietzsche himself. As Jaspers concluded of his philosophy, "Everything is up to us. Truth is only what Nietzsche brings out of ourselves" (Jaspers, 1961, p. 107). Read Nietzsche in order to one day overcome him, and go beyond him. As he wrote in *Ecce Homo*: "One repays a teacher badly if one remains only a pupil. And why, then, should you pluck at my laurels?" (EH Forward.4). One reads Nietzsche in order to ultimately reject him, to become what you are. Nietzsche preaches total freedom. Even from him. As he himself put it: "I have no use for disciples. Let everyone be his (and her) own true follower" (Fuss and Shapiro, 1971, p. 46).

Acknowledgements: My thanks to Mary Kenny, Joanna Williams, Maren Thom and Ed West for reading through versions of this book, for their suggestions, criticisms, corrections and encouragement. My thanks also for their help and encouragement to Tina Watkins, Gabriella Assante, Toni Pereira, Sarah Lovell and Sir Roger Scruton.

Friedrich Nietzsche's Works

The Birth of Tragedy (1872)
Slightly revised 2nd edition, 1878. New preface, 1886.
Untimely Meditations
David Strauss (1873)
On the Use and Disadvantage of History (1873)
Schopenhauer as Educator (1874)
Richard Wagner in Bayreuth (1876)
Human, All Too Human (1878)
Mixed Opinions and Maxims (1st sequel, 1879)
The Wanderer and His Shadow (2nd sequel, 1880)
Daybreak (1881)
Second edition (1887)
The Joyous Science (1882)
Second edition (1887)
Thus Spoke Zarathustra
Parts I and II published separately in 1883, Part III in 1884, Part IV in 1885
Beyond Good and Evil (1886)
On The Genealogy of Morals (1887)
The Twilight of the Idols (written 1888; 1889)
The Antichrist (written 1888; 1895)
The Case of Wagner (written 1888; 1895)
Ecce Homo (written 1888; 1905)
"The Will to Power" (Notes written 1883–88; 1901)

BIBLIOGRAPHY

Books by Friedrich Nietzsche

The Birth of Tragedy and the Case of Wagner, Translated, With Commentary, by Walter Kaufmann, Vintage Books, New York (1967)

Thoughts Out of Season, Translated by Anthony M. Ludovici, Part 1, TN Foulis, Edinburgh & London (1910)

Thoughts Out of Season, Translated by Adrian Collins, Part 2, TN Foulis, Edinburgh & London (1910)

Human, All Too Human, Translated by Marion Faber and Stephen Lehmann, Introduction and Notes by Marion Faber, Penguin, London (2004)

Daybreak, Thoughts on the Prejudices of Morality, Translated by R.J. Hollingdale, with an Introduction by Michael Tanner, Cambridge University Press, Cambridge (1982)

The Gay Science, with a prelude in rhymes and an appendix of songs, Translated, with Commentary, by Walter Kaufmann, Vintage Books, New York (1974)

Thus Spoke Zarathustra, A Book for Everyone and No One, Translated by R.J. Hollingdale, Penguin, London (1961, 1969)

Beyond Good and Evil, Prelude to a Philosophy of the Future, Translated by R.J. Hollingdale, with an Introduction by Michael Tanner, Penguin, London (1973, 1990)

On the Genealogy of Morals, Translated with an Introduction and Notes by Douglas Smith, Oxford University Press, Oxford (1996)

Twilight of the Idols/ The Anti-Christ, Translation and Translator's Note R.J. Hollingdale, Penguin, London (1968, 1990)

The Case of Wagner, Macmillan, New York (1911)

Ecce Homo, Translation by R.J. Hollingdale, 1979, new Introduction and text revisions by Michael Tanner, Penguin, London (1992)

The Will to Power: In Science, Nature, Society and Art, Translated by Walter Kaufmann and R.J. Hollingdale, Edited by Walter Kaufmann, Vintage Books, New York (1973)

Collected letters

Nietzsche: A Self-Portrait from His Letters, Edited and Translated by Peter Fuss and Henry Shapiro, Harvard University Press, Cambridge, MA (1971)

Friedrich Nietzsche, Selected Letters, Translated by A.N. Lucovici, Edited with an Introduction by O. Levy, Soho Book Company, London (1921, 1985)

Books on Nietzsche

Nietzsche's Middle Period, Ruth Abbey, Oxford University Press, Oxford (2000)

Nietzsche, Crane Brinton, Harvard University Press, Cambridge, MA (1941, 1948)

Friedrich Nietzsche, Curtis Cate, Hutchinson, London (2002)

Friedrich Nietzsche, Philosopher of Culture, Frederick Copleston SJ, Search Press, London (1942, 1975)

Nietzsche as Philosopher, Arthur C. Danto, Macmillan, New York (1965, 1968, 1970)

Nietzsche and Philosophy, Gilles Deleuze, Translated by Hugh Tomlinson, Athlone Press, London (1962, 1983)

The Will to Freedom, or The Gospel of Nietzsche and the Gospel of Christ, John Neville Figgis, Longmans, Green and Co, London (1917)

Le problème de la vérité dans la philosophie de Nietzsche, Jean Granier, Éditions du seuil, Paris (1966)

Nietzsche, A Critical Life, Ronald Hayman, Weidenfeld and Nicolson, London (1980)

The Importance of Nietzsche, Ten Essays, Erich Heller, University of Chicago Press, Chicago, IL (1988)

Nietzsche, The Man and His Philosophy, R.G. Hollingdale, 2nd edition, Ark books, London (1985)

Nietzsche and Christianity, Karl Jaspers, Translated by E.B. Ashton, Henry Regnery Company, Chicago, IL (1961)

Nietzsche, Philosopher, Psychologist, Antichrist, Walter Kaufmann, 4th edition, Princeton University Press, Princeton, NJ (1974)

Nietzsche, Heidegger, and Buber, Walter Arnold Kaufmann, McGraw-Hill, New York (1980)

The Quintessence of Nietzsche, J.M. Kennedy, T. Werner Laurie, London (1909)

The Tragic Philosopher, A Study of Friedrich Nietzsche, F.A. Lea, Methuen, London (1957)

Nietzsche on Morality, Brian Leiter, Routledge, London (2002)

Nietzsche, A Biographical Introduction, Janko Lavrin, Studio Vista, London (1971)

Who is to be Master of the World? An Introduction to the Philosophy of Friedrich Nietzsche, Anthony M. Ludovici, TN Foulis, Edinburgh (1914)

Friedrich Nietzsche, The Dionysian Spirit of the Age, A.R. Orage, TN Foulis, London and Edinburgh (1906)

Nietzsche: Disciple of Dionysus, Rose Pfeffer, Bucknell University Press, Lewisburg, PA (1972)

Nietzsche, A Philosophical Biography, Rüdiger Safranski, Translated by Shelley Frisch, Granta, London (2002)

Nietzsche and the Gods, Weaver Santaniello, Suny Press, Albany, NY (2001)

Nietzsche for Beginners, Marc Sautet, Illustrated by Patrick Boussignac, Writers and Readers, New York (1990)

Nietzsche's Postmoralism, Essays on Nietzsche's Prelude to Philosophy's Future, Edited by Richard Schacht, Cambridge University Press, Cambridge (2001)

Living with Nietzsche, What the Great 'Immoralist' Has to Teach Us, Robert C. Solomon, Oxford University Press, Oxford (2003)

Reading Nietzsche, Edited by Robert C. Solomon and Kathleen M. Higgins, Oxford University Press, Oxford (1988)

A Study of Nietzsche, J.P. Stern, Cambridge University Press, Cambridge (1979)

Nietzsche, Michael Tanner, Oxford University Press, Oxford (1994)

Nietzsche in England 1890–1914, The Growth of a Reputation, David S. Thatcher, University of Toronto Press, Toronto (1970)

Nietzsche, An Introduction, Gianni Vattimo, Translated by Nicholas Martin, Athlone Press, London (1985, 2002)

The Philosophy of Nietzsche, by A. Wolf, George Allen & Unwin, London (1915, 1923)

Nietzsche, A Re-Examination, Irving M. Zeitlin, Polity Press, Cambridge (1994)

Other secondary works

At the Existentialist Cafe, Sarah Bakewell, Chatto & Windus, London (2016)

The Consolations of Philosophy, Alain de Botton, Hamish Hamilton, London (2000)

The Rebel, Albert Camus, Translated by Anthony Bower and with an Afterword by Olivier Todd, 2000 (*L'Homme révolté*, 1951)

The Works of Charles Darwin, Volume 23: The Expression of the Emotions in Man and Animals, Charles Darwin, Sir Francis Darwin, Paul H. Barrett, R.B. Freeman, Routledge, London (1890, 2015)

Our Dumb Century, Edited by Scott Dikkers, Three Rivers Press, New York (1999)

The Essential Works of Michel Foucault, 1954–1984, Volume Three, Power, Penguin, London (1994, 2000)

Man's Search for Meaning, Viktor Frankl, Rider, London (1946, 1959, 2004)

Straw Dogs, Thoughts on Humans and other Animals, John Gray, Farrar, Straus and Giroux, New York (2003)

The De-Moralization of Society, From Victorian Virtues to Modern Values, Gertrude Himmelfarb, IEA Health and Welfare Unit, London (1995)

Egotists, A Book of Superman, James Huneker, Charles Scriber's Sons, New York (1909)

Experiments Against Reality, The fate of culture in the postmodern age, Roger Kimball, Ivan R Dee publishers, Chicago, IL (2000)

The Origins of the First World War, Great Power Rivalry and German War Aims, Edited by H.W. Koch, Palgrave Macmillan, London (1972, 1982)

Selfish, Whining Monkeys, How We Ended Up Greedy, Narcissistic and Unhappy, Rod Liddle, Fourth Estate, London (2014)

Autobiography, Morrissey, Penguin, London (2013)

Harry Potter and the Philosopher's Stone, J.K. Rowling, Bloomsbury, London (1997)

History of Western Philosophy, and its Connection with Political and Social Circumstances from the Earliest Times to the Present Day, Bertrand Russell, George Allen & Unwin, London (1946, 1962)

The Rise and Fall of The Third Reich, William L. Shirer, Simon & Schuster, New York (1960)

The Essential Schopenhauer, Unwin Books, London (1962)

Modern Philosophy, A Survey, Roger Scruton, Sinclair-Stevenson, London (1994)

Fools, Frauds and Firebrands, Roger Scruton, Bloomsbury, London (2015)

A Short History of Modern Philosophy, From Descartes to Wittgenstein, 2nd edition, Roger Scruton, Routledge, London (1981, 1995, 2002)

The Icon Critical Dictionary of Postmodern Thought, Edited by Stuart Sim, Allen & Unwin, London (1998)

Philosophy, 100 Essential Thinkers, Philip Stokes, Enchanted Lion Books, New York (2005)

The Passion of the Western Mind, Understanding the Ideas that Have Shaped Our World View, Richard Tarnas, Ballantine Books, New York (1991)

The Age of Nothing, How We Have Sought to Live Since the Death of God, Peter Watson, Weidenfeld & Nicolson, London (2014, 2016)

Conspicuous Compassion, Patrick West, Civitas, London (2004)

Academic Freedom in an Age of Conformity, Confronting the Fear of Knowledge, Joanna Williams, Palgrave Macmillan, Basingstoke (2016)

Carry On Jeeves, P.G. Wodehouse, Barrie and Jenkins, London (1925)

The Generation of 1914, Robert Wohl, Weidenfeld and Nicolson, London (1980)

Index